IMPACTS
OF NATIONAL
TECHNOLOGY
PROGRAMMES

ORGANISATION FOR ECONOMIC CO-OPERATION AND DEVELOPMENT

ORGANISATION FOR ECONOMIC CO-OPERATION AND DEVELOPMENT

Pursuant to Article 1 of the Convention signed in Paris on 14th December 1960, and which came into force on 30th September 1961, the Organisation for Economic Co-operation and Development (OECD) shall promote policies designed:

— to achieve the highest sustainable economic growth and employment and a rising standard of living in Member countries, while maintaining financial stability, and thus to contribute to the development of the world economy;

— to contribute to sound economic expansion in Member as well as non-member countries in the process of economic development; and

— to contribute to the expansion of world trade on a multilateral, non-discriminatory basis in accordance with international obligations.

The original Member countries of the OECD are Austria, Belgium, Canada, Denmark, France, Germany, Greece, Iceland, Ireland, Italy, Luxembourg, the Netherlands, Norway, Portugal, Spain, Sweden, Switzerland, Turkey, the United Kingdom and the United States. The following countries became Members subsequently through accession at the dates indicated hereafter: Japan (28th April 1964), Finland (28th January 1969), Australia (7th June 1971), New Zealand (29th May 1973) and Mexico (18th May 1994). The Commission of the European Communities takes part in the work of the OECD (Article 13 of the OECD Convention).

Publié en français sous le titre :

LES INCIDENCES DES PROGRAMMES TECHNOLOGIQUES NATIONAUX

Foreword

Government support for science and technology (S&T) is pervasive. In aggregate, governments finance a major part of national Research and Development (R&D) but R&D is only part of this support. Moreoever, R&D represents only one part of the innovation system.

Governments have various justifications for supporting S&T programmes, most of which are difficult to translate into formal economic terms. Nevertheless, governments must provide economic analysis of programmes, especiall those with specific economic objectives.

Economic evaluation of specific S&T programmes is necessarily problematic. There are difficult counterfactual (what if) problems. More important, there are significant scientific and commercial uncertainties, and programmes acquire lives of their own. Still more important, government intervention (even with specific S&T programmes) is only part of a wider (national and international) innovation system, and assessing the impacts of a specific government role is difficult.

This study reviews the issues of impact evaluation, and introduces results from a wide range of *ex post* evaluations of government S&T programmes. It considers various forms of government intervention (fiscal support/direct subsidies) and the role of targeting particular objectives.

This study was prepared by Martin Brown of the OECD's Directorate for Science, Technology and Industry. It is published on the responsibility of the Secretary-General of the OECD.

Table of contents

List of tables

Executive summary

This paper is concerned with the impacts of the portion of national government support for technology innovation and diffusion that can be represented in terms of specific programmes which have been evaluated. Most government R&D programmes are only partly about promoting innovation and industrial competitiveness.

Chapter 1 takes up the matter of justification. The traditional economic justification for government intervention is market failure. The TEP analysis, however, suggests wider criteria: new growth theories, the innovation process, national innovation systems and globalisation. Further potential justifications include:

i) technology for social, non-economic goals;
ii) "distributive" criteria;
iii) promotion of "critical" technologies; and
iv) response to other countries' programmes.

Chapter 2 attempts to classify programmes. Most involve multiple objectives and instruments.

Chapter 3 considers evaluation. Most evaluation has concerned public accountability and programme management. The "institutionalisation" of efficient processes has become a key question. Longer-term impacts are particularly difficult to identify and assess. Intermediate indicators are needed.

Chapter 4 reviews impacts of national technology programmes as reflected in available empirical results of evaluation. The last Chapter summarises the main conclusions of the report. Economic evaluation of impacts is problematic, and is not adequately covered in most formal evaluations. Evaluation bias is a very real problem. Targeted programmes carry considerable (especially commercial) risks. In some countries, overall efforts have been dominated by a few programmes. The evidence on indirect fiscal programmes is fairly inconclusive but, on balance, positive.

In terms of promoting successful innovation and (especially) targeting, the record of government intervention is mixed. Most evaluations report significant successes. Some underline the catalyst role of government in bringing together partners and launching programmes. However, a few point to dramatic failures in picking winners, and to the difficulties governments may encounter in efficiently pursuing innovation beyond the "pre-competitive" stage.

As regards national innovation systems and technology diffusion, the results are inconclusive. Pre-competitive programmes have promoted networking in collaborative R&D. Some SME programmes report considerable success.

In the case of international programmes and issues, interpretation of evaluation results is especially difficult. Most evaluations point to significant benefits. There may be a trade-off between promoting national competitiveness and obtaining economies of scale in and access to international programmes. Most evaluations of international collaborative programmes have found successful outcomes, but a few have raised questions about the ''distributive'' aspects.

Introduction

In the current discussion of OECD countries' technology policies, a key topic is the role and effectiveness of governments in promoting national technology programmes. Questions have also been raised as to whether government support has an effect on national competitiveness and, if so, whether that support is appropriate.

This report examines various aspects of impact evaluation as applied to identifiable national technology programmes, *i.e.* specific programmes to support industrial technology.[1] It should be understood from the outset that these programmes are only a part of national innovation systems (NIS) – the part that concerns explicit government intentions. Moreover, "identifiable" is very much the operative word here, since government influence on the innovation process can extend far beyond assessable programmes. In (greatly) simplifying the notion of support, there is a very real danger of distorting the discussion of technology policy.

Thus the focus is necessarily narrowed. First of all, precisely what is meant by "technology programme"? The discussion in Chapter 1 centres on government support to pre-competitive and near-market R&D, whose performance involves governments and the enterprise sector. However, it is recognised that there is no clear definition of "pre-competitive" or "near-market" R&D, since technology innovation and diffusion is not a linear process from basic research to commercial application. The wider concept that emerged from OECD's Technology and the Economy Programme (TEP) analysis (OECD, 1992a, outlined here in Chapter 1) thus serves as the basis for the rest of the report.[2] Chapter 2 considers different criteria for classifying these programmes for purposes of analysis.

By focusing on specific technology programmes, the research can more fully address programme methodologies, which are still tentative and fragmentary, and practical analyses of their impacts. Most evaluation is driven by concerns about public accountability (financial and administrative), and does not relate well to the technology policy notions developed in Chapters 1 and 4. Chapter 3 emphasises economic criteria in evaluation, and retains the central counterfactual criterion for impact evaluation: how different was the actual outcome from what would have happened without the programme?

At the same time, it is important to recognise that focusing on specific programmes may well bias any overall assessments of the impacts of national technology efforts; the programmes in fact represent a small, if significant, part of these efforts. Limiting the discussion to those programmes that have been evaluated introduces a further – and, for the present, largely unpredictable – bias. Evaluation involves significant costs and so could be applied more readily to large or politically-visible programmes. Moreover, since most evaluation is a consensual activity which seeks to institutionalise and legitimise itself, there may be a bias towards finding positive results.

Chapter 1

Government's role in national innovation systems: extent and justification

Introduction

Most government R&D programme objectives only partly concern the promotion of innovation and industrial competitiveness. This chapter examines the overall allocation of national R&D in an effort to identify the share that can be considered as "dedicated" to specific programmes to promote industrial technology and competitiveness.

Government intervention to support innovation requires justification. That fact is central to policy discussion; however, it is also of practical importance because most assessments of programme impacts data are conducted in relation to programme objectives, which are closely tied to justification. There are a number of possible justifications, which are reviewed in this chapter.

Quantitative data on industrial R&D programmes

What follows is a "snapshot" picture of the most recent internationally-comparable aggregate data available on pre-competitive and near-market R&D, which will place the discussion of national technology programmes in a clearer context. There is no attempt to analyse the data, which come mainly from the OECD's STIID data bank, or to provide exhaustive coverage; rather, country/regional differences are examined, along with some recent developments.

The main concern here is with the role of governments and with innovation, neither of which is straightforward. First, a major portion of government efforts (and programmes) in relation to technology and innovation is not adequately reflected in government R&D, whether financing or performing (*e.g.* fiscal incentives to enterprise R&D, government procurement). Secondly, technology and innovation activities are not easily identified in terms of socio-economic objectives or types of activity.

The OECD's analysis of R&D activities distinguishes between financing and performing. Basically, there are two primary sources of data on industrial R&D:

- government appropriations (financing) by socio-economic objectives, shown in Table 1 for the main categories which concern industrial innovation; and

Table 1. Government budget appropriations for R&D socio-economic objectives

Percentage of total government R&D appropriations, 1993

	Industrial development	Energy	Transport	Civil space	Defence
Australia	12.2	2.3	1.2	..	9.5
Austria	7.7	0.9	1.8	0.0	0.0
Belgium	11.8	2.9	..	13.5	0.2
Canada[1]	10.8	5.8	3.6	6.0	7.3
Denmark[2]	11.7	4.0	..	3.1	0.6
Finland	30.9	3.8	2.9	2.5	1.6
France[2]	7.5	3.9	..	9.8	34.6
Germany[2]	13.3	4.7	0.4	5.9	10.5
Greece[2]	10.0	2.3	..	0.3	2.4
Iceland[2]	5.9	9.1	1.9	..	0.0
Ireland	25.1	0.3	0.0	0.4	0.0
Italy	16.3	4.0	..	6.4	6.5
Netherlands	15.6	3.2	2.1	4.0	3.5
New Zealand[2]	12.5	1.2	1.1	0.1	1.3
Norway	12.9	3.3	5.1	2.5	5.0
Portugal	18.3	4.3	..	0.3	0.4
Spain	20.2	2.1	0.6	7.0	11.9
Sweden[2]	6.3	2.4	5.3	1.4	24.3
Switzerland[1]	8.2	3.9	8.0	..	18.5
Turkey	n.a.	n.a.	n.a.	n.a.	n.a.
United Kingdom	8.5	1.9	..	3.3	45.1
United States	0.3	3.8	2.5	9.8	59.2
Japan	3.9	21.3	1.5	7.1	5.9
North America[1]	0.7	4.5	1.9	9.7	57.6
EC-12[2]	14.7	3.9	0.3	6.3	20.7
Nordic countries[2]	12.8	3.3	4.1	1.9	12.2
Total OECD[1]	6.4	5.8	1.4	7.8	38.3

1. 1991.
2. 1992.
Source: OECD/EASD (STIU database), March 1994.

– expenditures (performance) coming from surveys of enterprises compiled by governments; reflected in Tables 2-4.

It is important to note the limitations of the data. In the government appropriations category, there are problems concerning the inclusion of fiscal expenditures, procurement and government equity. In the enterprise surveys, the data do not distinguish between direct supports to enterprise R&D and government contracts in general; furthermore, they do not include indirect supports (fiscal, soft loans, guarantees and equity capital).

Government appropriations specifically targeted for industrial development are only a small part of overall appropriations supporting industrial innovation, and an even

Table 2. **Share of business enterprise R&D financed by government**

Percentage

	1981	1985	1989	1991
Australia	8.4	6.9	2.7	2.6
Austria	7.4	7.9	5.6	..
Belgium	8.3	8.4	6.0	..
Canada	10.7	12.0	10.0	9.6
Denmark	12.4	9.9	11.7	7.9
Finland	4.2	3.2	3.1	5.4
France	24.6	23.4	19.3	22.3
Germany	16.9	15.3	11.0	10.7[1]
Greece	4.6	14.7	8.6	5.5
Iceland	38.3	15.8	10.9	9.6
Ireland	13.7	12.4	6.9	3.7
Italy	8.8	16.9	16.3	11.8
Japan	1.9	1.6	1.2	1.4
Netherlands	7.5	12.6	10.6	7.5
New Zealand	16.4	n.a.	6.5[1]	6.2
Norway	25.3	18.8	19.6	15.9
Portugal	1.6[2]	2.9[3]	4.5	..
Spain	4.1	7.7	11.8	11.3
Sweden	13.6	11.6	12.6	11.5
Switzerland	1.3	1.8[4]	0.8	..
Turkey	n.a.	n.a.	n.a.	..
United Kingdom	30.0	23.0	17.2	14.6
United States	31.6	32.3	30.7	24.8

1. Break in series.
2. 1982.
3. Average 1984-86.
4. 1986.

Source: OECD, EASD database, March 1994.

smaller part of total government R&D efforts (Table 1). In 1991, they amounted to
somewhat less than 6 per cent. The OECD estimated (1989*a,* Figure 16) that the overall
shares for Member countries in the past decade were as follows (percentage of total):

defence	–40
civil	–60
of which: General University Funds	–9
health	–15
civil space	–9
advancement of research	–45
economic development	–45
(of which industry and energy had 15 each)	

Table 3. **Share of total government-financed R&D performed by business enterprises**

Percentage

	1981	1985	1989	1991
Australia	2.9	3.8	2.9	2.3[5]
Austria	8.8	9.0	7.6	..
Belgium	21.5[2]	19.1	14.9	..
Canada	10.4	13.4	12.2	11.7
Denmark	11.6	11.8	14.1	11.6
Finland	5.3	5.4	5.4	7.6
France	27.2	26.0	24.1	28.1
Germany	29.1	30.5	23.3	20.3[6]
Greece	1.3	5.7[3]	2.8	2.5
Iceland	4.3	3.8	3.2	3.0
Ireland	10.6	13.8	11.5	8.1
Italy	10.5	18.6	19.4	14.8
Japan[7]	5.0	6.2	5.5	..
Netherlands	8.4	16.0	15.0	8.9
New Zealand	4.3	n.a.	3.3[6]	3.0[5]
Norway	23.4	26.0	21.8	17.5
Portugal	0.8[1]	1.3	1.8	..
Spain	3.3	8.9	14.2	13.9
Sweden	20.5	21.8	21.7	22.2
Switzerland	4.0	6.7[4]	2.7	..
Turkey	n.a.	n.a.	n.a.	..
United Kingdom	39.3	34.0	32.5	27.9
United States	45.1	48.5	45.8	37.7

1. 1982.
2. 1983.
3. 1986.
4. 1988.
5. 1990.
6. Break in series.
7. Adjusted by Secretariat.
Source: OECD, EASD database, March 1994.

Thus, the overall share is determined mostly by appropriations for defence. These appropriations are essentially for industrial development, and are reflected in Tables 2 to 4.[3] The countries with the highest share of defence spending are the United States (59 per cent), France (37 per cent), the United Kingdom (44 per cent) and Sweden (27 per cent). In terms of overall OECD 1991 appropriations for defence, the shares were (approximately): United States – 75 per cent, France – 11 per cent, United Kingdom – 7 per cent, Germany – 3 per cent, Japan and Sweden – 1 per cent. The share of defence appropriations, while still high, is declining sharply. This is important for the evaluation of national technology programmes and policy discussion: non-industrial programmes are not well recorded and cannot easily be evaluated, but have nonetheless led to the growing

Table 4. **Share of government in enterprise R&D**

Percentage of total R&D

(1991 or nearest year available)

	Electricals	Chemicals	Aerospace	Transport	Basic metals	Machinery	Total manufacturing
Australia	3.1	0.7	42.9	0.3	1.2	3.2	2.6
Austria[1]	3.1	4.1	..	1.5	4.9	3.7	3.6
Belgium	..	..	..	..	..	..	..
Canada	..	..	..	..	..	..	..
Denmark	4.5	2.4	..	1.3	2.1	2.8	3.7
Finland	7.2	..	..	..	9.8	7.2	5.5
France[2]	31.2	4	0	1.1	2.7	12.9	20.6
Germany[1]	7.4	1.7	..	1.2	18.8	5.0	9.8
Greece	..	..	..	..	..	..	..
Iceland[2]	3.5	3.9	..	..	..	9.1	3.9
Ireland[2]	5.0	4	0	39	15.9	4.0	5.1
Italy	18.7	1.2	45.3	5.4	13.8	15.4	15.2
Japan[1]	0.7	0.7	9.0	3.7	0.9	0.6	1.2
Netherlands	..	..	..	..	..	..	10
New Zealand	..	..	..	..	..	..	..
Norway	7.6	0.5	4	13.6	4.2	27.0	9.7
Portugal	..	..	..	..	..	..	..
Spain	7.3	1.6	10.3	7.5	16.6	10.5	8.6
Sweden	7.9	0.6	..	20.9	4.1	15.5	10.3
Switzerland	..	..	..	..	..	..	..
Turkey	..	..	..	..	..	..	..
United Kingdom[1]	20.6	0.7	39.3	1.7	17.5	13.6	14.8
United States	31.1	0.8	76.5	19.0	10.9	..	30.7

1. 1989.
2. 1990.
Source: OECD, EASD database, March 1994.

number of "spin-off/dual-use" programmes, especially in the United States (Alic *et al.,* 1992, and Branscomb, 1993 and 1994).

For the other Member countries, the share of government appropriations for industrial development is typically between 10 and 20 per cent. However, as Table 1 shows, the share of categories such as energy, transport and civil space, which are primarily about industrial innovation, is significant in most countries. It should be noted that other socio-economic objectives (about 40 per cent of the OECD total) may be relevant to industrial innovation (especially agriculture and public health).

In terms of performance, about 10 per cent (the median) of enterprise R&D is financed by government (Table 2), and a somewhat higher share of government-financed R&D is performed by the enterprise sector (Table 3).

Defence expenditures are clearly a determining factor in the shares, with a very large portion of enterprise sector R&D financed by government. In the United States, the share of the 1989 total was 31 per cent, in France 19 per cent, and in the United Kingdom 17 per cent. The strong share increase in Spain, from 4.1 per cent in 1981 to 11.8 per cent in 1989, is probably also defence-driven.

Public ownership of the industrial sector is an important factor in the shares and trends. There have been major reductions in the shares of business enterprise R&D financed by the government in most OECD countries (Table 2), and especially in the United Kingdom, France and Germany. These reductions may represent partly the "privatisation" of public R&D capabilities, and partly the continuing high levels of public ownership in some countries (*e.g.* Norway). However, in principle, the STIID's database, which comes from enterprise surveys, should not distinguish between public and private ownership of enterprises.

Government support for enterprise R&D is much higher in some industrial sectors. Nevertheless, the picture that comes from Tables 1 to 4 suggests that *overall* direct government support for enterprise industrial R&D is modest, although there are significant differences between countries.

More generally, the STIID tables support the analysis presented below, which suggests that government support for enterprise R&D is pervasive but does not, in the aggregate, represent more than a small (if significant) part of enterprise effort. Most of this government effort is not earmarked for industrial development. As stated in the Introduction, specific programmes for industrial innovation represent only a very small portion of overall government efforts.

However, the statistical data pose a major problem with regard to both spin-offs from government R&D which are not dedicated to industrial development, and (increasingly) "dual-use" technology programmes. These cannot be captured in the aggregate statistics, and present methodological difficulties (Chapter 2) and policy problems (Chapter 4). Nevertheless, they have been a central part of (implicit) national technology programmes, and are becoming more important in financial and policy terms.

Justification for public industrial R&D

National technology programmes of the type reviewed in this paper need to be justified. In formal administrative and political terms, they have to state objectives. The discussion below suggests that the most frequent scenario is a mixture of precise, vague, and – in some cases – conflicting objectives. The stated objectives reflect a need to justify government intervention in an area where such intervention is not the driver of most R&D and technology innovation. The justification comes from various arguments which raise policy issues. Moreover, in practical terms, most evaluation of impacts is conducted in relation to the stated objectives.

Economic justifications

From a neo-classical perspective, government intervention to support enterprise R&D is justified in national economic terms only if: *i)* the enterprise sector would not otherwise undertake the R&D, *i.e.* there is "market failure"; *ii)* there are nevertheless reasonable prospects that the R&D will lead to commercially-profitable products or processes; and *iii)* the overall cost/benefit calculations, with allowance for "technological spillovers" and possible negative effects (*e.g.* the crowding out of other R&D), are positive.[4]

There can be various market failure reasons why enterprises should fail to finance R&D programmes which have reasonable prospects of commercial viability. They are frequently classified as involving:

  i) Externalities: firms cannot "appropriate" the full social benefits of R&D investment as private financial gains.
  ii) Indivisibilities: the minimum size of R&D investment required is too great for the financing resources of individual firms.
  iii) Risks: the risks of failure with the proposed R&D are too great for any individual firm to accept, but would be acceptable for a government with a much larger overall investment portfolio, or one with wider priorities.

On externalities, in the simplest case, a firm cannot recover the costs of R&D for the innovation because other firms could imitate the new process or product without bearing the start-up innovation costs. This could be because the innovating firm cannot establish adequate intellectual property rights (IPR) over its innovation, or cannot establish sufficient commercial lead time over its competitors to recoup its innovatory investment.

The indivisibilities justification for government intervention raises difficult questions – especially for "near-market" research – about competition policy and collaboration in R&D between dominant firms. This is linked to the appropriability issues discussed below: there is a trade-off between a desire to retain technology development and diffusion within the public domain (through public support for R&D) and efficient development (perhaps involving changes in competition policy).

Risks may be technological or commercial. The evidence indicates that they are primarily commercial (Cohen and Noll, 1991; Toulemonde, 1990). Both types of risk may justify government intervention, but commercial risks raise wider policy issues as well as questions about the extent to which policies other than R&D support would have been more appropriate. Nevertheless, the fact that a government was willing to take a risk that industry declined does not mean that the government was wrong if the process or product fails to be commercially successful: governments generally have larger portfolios than individual firms.

Market failure is a signal that the national economic/social returns to R&D expenditures may be higher than the private financial returns; studies show that this is indeed the case (through spillovers), but that there is a very wide dispersion of results between sectors. Justification for government intervention to promote R&D is thus clearly established. However, the central evaluation problem is to ascertain: *i)* how far government

17

programmes induce additional R&D; *ii)* how far additional R&D captures benefits for the national economy (how far are the benefits of government-sponsored R&D comparable to those of enterprise R&D in general?); and *iii)* which policy instruments (*e.g.* how much targeting?) are best adapted to promote successful national economic outcomes.

Branscomb (1993, p. 72) suggests for the United States the six most frequently encountered types of market failures which may justify government intervention. These are:

- basic research in areas of science supporting a firm's core competencies and exchanged freely with scientists and engineers in industry and universities (such as chaos theory, mathematics);
- pathbreaking technologies with the potential to create new industries or product clusters, but with high risks and long payback periods (such as fusion power, electric cars, high-temperature superconductivity);
- infrastructural technologies and technology-motivated science with broad application throughout industry in which the payback is relatively certain and rapid, but whose economic value to any single firm is only weakly appropriable (such as design-automation tools, materials characterisation, properties of matter and materials, non-destructive test methods, and physical and chemical data compilations);
- technologies serving markets with high barriers to entry, such as those whose entry costs exceed what private capital markets will support given the extended time required to recover the initial investment (SST, MagLev trains, etc.);
- strategic technologies, where markets are too small or too cyclical to sustain the technological infrastructure required for viability of an important domestic industry (such as the semiconductor manufacturing tool-makers supported by SemaTech); and
- technologies for mixed public/private markets, where public policy issues have the effect of increasing private risks (such as molecular biology and the intelligent highways system), or where public values justify an acceleration of development effort beyond what the market will elicit (such as environmentally-superior processes).

In parallel, there is a growing body of research and policy discussion about the appropriability of innovation activities, which offers insights for the justification and evaluation of national technology programmes (Hanel and Palda, 1992; Levin *et al.,* 1987). The notion of appropriability can be usefully applied to the market failure discussion: externalities or spillovers are social returns to innovating activities which cannot be "appropriated" by the firm.

Appropriability is also pertinent to discussions of the innovation process. In what is now recognised to be a caricature of the process, innovation is driven by "basic research" through various stages of "pre-competitive" research towards "near-market" research and the development of new products and processes. In this over-simplified linear process, the earlier phases are not (and should not be) appropriable – the resulting knowledge is a public good whose consumption is "non-rival" – and this is a legitimate area for government financing. As the process moves towards the market, the appropriability issue causes greater concern, and government intervention needs more justification. It can be argued that governments should extend the area of "non-appropriability" (in which knowledge is a public good). This would provide the justification for promoting industrial competition. The corollary is that they should fund the R&D; this has been the justification for national technology programmes to fund pre-competitive research.[5]

The major problem with this linear notion of innovation associated with the idea of "technology-push" is that it simply does not correspond to reality. Much innovation is "demand-pulled" – with the market doing the pulling – and, importantly, involves an interactive process between basic and applied research. There is also considerable evidence that firms can appropriate the social benefits of basic research, which complicates the typology of programmes. The justification for government intervention therefore becomes much more complicated, as does the evaluation of impacts.

Two further points should be noted about appropriability and the evaluation of government programmes:

   i) there are major empirical questions about appropriability analysis; and
   ii) there is a difficult problem about who acquires the intellectual property rights from government-financed programmes.

Transaction costs represent a further source of market failure (a strong argument from the European perspective – see Watkins, 1991). These include the costs of communicating technical knowledge, especially for requisite in-house technological capability. Ergas (1993) argues that, with French programmes, while transaction costs are reduced through "cultural" factors (associated with the education of elites), the costs in terms of programme performance have been considerable.

Market failure is also linked to certain categories of public goods produced from technology. Conceptually, technology outputs can be distinguished in terms of the extent to which they are rival or non-rival and "exclusive". Table 5, from Romer (1993), illustrates how different outputs can be placed within these two dimensions. The first dimension reflects the costs of their development and production; the second is concerned with the extent to which the developers (or governments) can control their use. Fully private goods are both rival (just one person can enjoy their use) and exclusive (property rights are fully effective). Completely public goods are non-rival (the marginal cost of reproducing them is negligible) and there is little ownership/control over their use. Market failure occurs when falling marginal costs make products non-rival and/or when innovators cannot control the use of their innovations. Government support for technology can seek to meet market failure by shifting the location of outputs within these two dimensions.

However, government objectives may not be consistent. Within the rivalry dimension, governments can only seek to shift the outcomes towards non-rival outputs (by financing fixed costs of R&D). On the exclusivity/control front, they can seek to correct for market failure either by strengthening ownership (mainly through intellectual property rights) or by shifting R&D outputs into the public domain. It is important to recognise that these are conflicting objectives.

19

Table 5. **Economic attributes of different goods**

	Rival goods (*e.g.* objects)	Non-rival goods (*e.g.* bit strings)
Degree of control or excludability 100%	Private goods: *e.g.* a piece of unimproved land	An encoded satellite television broadcast
		A digital music recording
		The design for a microprocessor
	A car	Computer code
		The operations manual for Wal-Mart stores
	A worker's labour effort	General principles of chemical engineering
		Principles behind widow-based graphical user interfaces
		The do-loop in computer programming
	Fish in the sea	
	Clean air	Public goods: *e.g.* basic research in physics
	Sterile insects used for pest control	
0%		

Source: Romer, 1993.

There can also be market failure to invest in R&D due to the long time-scales involved in bringing products and processes to the commercial market-place and to firms' assessment of risks in relation to different sources of finance for corporate R&D (Hall, 1992). It has frequently been argued that enterprises (especially in the United States) have been so motivated by short-term investment considerations that their implicit discount rate for investment, especially in industrial R&D, is much higher than any realistic longer-term national rate. Governments can afford to take a longer view. There are thus important system differences that can influence international competition. Tyson (1992, p. 286) argues that higher capital costs in the United Sates place small R&D-intensive firms at a competitive disadvantage *vis-à-vis* Japanese firms (*e.g.* in advanced display technology).

Thus, measures to correct for "market failure" do not necessarily entail government finance for R&D, whether direct or indirect. As noted above, externalities can be mitigated by intellectual property rights or secrecy, and governments can strengthen this protection. Commercially, there may be questions about industry structure and markets – governments can tolerate oligopolistic or monopolistic situations which allow firms to appropriate the returns to innovation investment. Public procurement has traditionally been an important policy instrument for this. Similarly, "indivisibility" market failures may result from government competition policies, in which case derogations from these could be an appropriate instrument (Branscomb, 1992). Market failures due to excessive risk may be amenable to financial policies. Thus, national technology programmes need to defend themselves against the possible policy alternatives for meeting market failure (McKeon and Ryan, 1989).

The TEP analysis (OECD, 1992a) introduced several strands into the discussion of technology innovation and diffusion which are not easily accommodated in the traditional neo-classical analysis. Four ideas in particular are relevant to the assessment of national technology programmes.

First, "new" growth theories assign an especially important role to investment in R&D, the returns to which are (from this perspective) much higher than those to other investment (or, implicitly, than market returns); accordingly, these theories suggest that macroeconomic policies should seek to raise the share of R&D in GDP. The evaluation criteria here concern the extent to which government programmes increase aggregate levels of R&D: they could simply substitute for enterprise R&D. Results are discussed in Chapter 4 below.

Secondly, the innovation process is not straightforward or random; there are important economies of scale along the learning curve, and "technological trajectories" can play a role. Thus it is legitimate for governments to try to pick "winners" from the competing technologies. With appropriate government support, some could indeed become commercial winners, with national firms moving down the learning curve into commercial success and with resulting national externalities and spillovers. This is an extension of the "risk" justification for government intervention. The principal issue for evaluation is governments' efficiency in picking winners and seeing them through to commercial success. For example, it was probably clear from the beginning that the global market would not be large enough to sustain commercially all the nuclear power technologies that were developed from the 1960s. What is relevant here is how governments perceived the risks they were underwriting and, still more, how they conducted and terminated the different programmes.[6] Chapter 4 suggests that governments' track record in picking winners is not good, but that a very few winners may be worth many losers. However, when "risk" justification is involved, evaluation should consider the whole programme portfolio – losers as well as winners.

Thirdly, "innovation systems/networks" are a key element in successful innovation and diffusion. In their national technology programmes, governments should be concerned with promoting a "healthy" development of the relevant innovation network as well as specific technologies – and, in particular, with supporting diffusion of technology to "small" actors (SMEs and universities). Most Member countries have (more or less specific) R&D support programmes for SMEs (see OECD, 1993). In some cases, there may also be an explicit objective to promote technology networks, especially closer links between national public laboratories/universities and industry (as in Australia, France and the United States). There seem to be three clear evaluation problems here. First, are all networking achievements equally positive? There may be alternatives. Secondly, how

21

durable are the achievements? Thirdly, to what extent should durability (as opposed to flexibility, for example) be a programme objective?[7]

One principle mentioned with regard to correcting market failure applies here: support for national innovation systems need not take the form of public finance of technology diffusion. Support for a strategic technology and a few innovators stimulates its own diffusion process. Also, there may be other, more appropriate policy instruments. However, this does make the task of "impacts" evaluation much more difficult, because the impacts to be assessed will not be confined to the principal actors in the programmes. It also adds unwelcome variables to the analysis of competition policy, both nationally and internationally, because these policy discussions and measures can easily focus only on the main participants in a programme.

Finally, the TEP emphasis on "globalisation" of economic activities and technology innovation calls in question simple notions such as the "nationality" of the actors involved and (therefore) national competitiveness. It raises, moreover, questions regarding access to national and international programmes, and poses problems for small and more technologically-backward countries.

It should be noted that the TEP analysis did not go much further than examining the issues and evidence and pointing to the potential policy implications. In particular, it did not endorse the new growth theories; the general implication was that the share of R&D in total investment and GDP should be raised. The TEP analysis also underlined that R&D is only one part of the innovation/diffusion process. Formal technology programmes are also just one of a range of policy instruments that governments use to promote national competitiveness.

It should be emphasised that government support to R&D does not take place in a perfectly competitive environment. Much of it is focused on areas characterised by oligopolistic and increasingly global competition. The neo-classical tradition, which underpins much of the discussion about support implicitly assumes that all the actors are well informed about what is happening, that they make profit-maximising decisions, that there are decreasing returns to scale, and that the individual actors are too small to influence the overall outcomes. New growth theories suggest that there may indeed be increasing returns to scale over an important part of the competitive life of a technology innovation. There are large and small actors, who interact differently with governments; large actors compete among themselves with variable strategies, both nationally and internationally, and this includes R&D strategy. Importantly, in some sectors, individual firms' R&D strategies may reflect assessments of other firms' strategies. The ability to appropriate technology innovations and to limit spillovers is one strategic weapon, but there are others, including "prime mover" advantages and government procurement. Individual firm R&D strategies may be either aggressive or defensive, and either case could involve socially-wasteful competitive R&D.

In this oligopolistic technology competition, governments intervene as individual players, but with objectives that are different from those of the other players. However, the thrust of this report is that, outside the defence sector, they are not (and cannot be) dominant players; in fact, their R&D strategies and consequent interventions are, to a considerable extent, a response to the strategies of the more dominant players. This accentuates the problems relating to government targeting of technology support, its evaluation, and the policy implications.

Other justifications for national technology programmes

There are a variety of justifications for programmes apart from the explicitly economic ones outlined above.

There is a general justification for public R&D if the eventual outputs will support social, non-economic goals ("technology for public goods"). Here, the argument is about supporting R&D which would lead to commercial applications but for which the market would depend on wider non-commercial government objectives, such as defence, public health or infrastructure (Hanel and Palda, 1992). In economic terms, there should still be discussion about why the innovations cannot/should not be appropriated by firms, and about the extent to which publicly-funded R&D programmes are the most appropriate policy instrument.

Spillovers/spin-offs pose an evaluation problem for some programmes. In general, they are part of the classical "externalities" justification for government intervention. The literature distinguishes two types of technological spin-off: technologies embodied in marketable products and knowledge externalities (Griliches, 1990; Bach *et al.*, 1992). Attempts (reviewed below) have been made to quantify them econometrically at the sector or macroeconomic level, but this yields little guidance for the evaluation of particular programmes, especially those with "public goods" justifications (Capron, 1992, p. 104). Most government technology programmes have specific objectives, for which spillovers would be a bonus. A few have spillovers (or dual-use technologies) as a primary objective. In the latter cases, technology development is in effect treated as sunk costs and the programme is concerned with better diffusion and use of acquired technologies or technologies being developed for other purposes (see Alic *et al.*, 1992 and, for nuclear technologies, NEA, 1993).

The evaluation problem is that only spillovers from clearly discrete programmes can be identified and measured. This could bias conclusions in favour of this type of programme. The more intractable policy difficulty concerns justifying and evaluating programmes which are "spun off" from other programmes that are justified for quite different reasons. This is compounded by the current policy objective to move from spin-offs to "spin-ons" (NAS, NAE, IOM, 1992; Alic *et al.*, 1992).

In some cases there are distributive criteria, *e.g.* an intention to support particular regional interests or threatened industries. The DISP shows some of these cases (*e.g.*shipbuilding), and others for which non-R&D objectives are "principal" yet support to R&D is the principal cost. The US Synfuel programme was very much dominated by regional interests (essentially, support for the East Coast coal industry – see NAS, NAE and IOM, 1992 and Cohen and Noll, 1991). The AIRDIS programme in Australia listed a special category of "public interest projects" (DITC, 1991*a* and *b*).

Distributive criteria can also apply to international collaborative R&D programmes, particularly those of the EC and EUREKA. Here, there may be important trade-offs between programme success and ensuring a "satisfactory" distribution of benefits in national terms – *le juste retour* (Olds, 1992). It has been argued that small, technologically-backward countries have been disadvantaged in the absence of distributive criteria (Tsipouri, 1991).

On the other hand, it has been argued that the European approach of promoting flexible R&D collaboration has, after an early derailment partly due to questions of national contributions and returns, developed an *à la carte* approach which satisfies national aspirations of participants within efficient programmes (Watkins, 1991).

A principal objective in a large number of national programmes has been the promotion of "strategic", "generic", "new" or "critical" technologies whose success is seen as eventually having widespread effects on industrial competitiveness. This category primarily involves information technologies (IT), biotechnology and new materials technologies. Here, the justification is primarily couched in terms of technology (see Alvey, 1991 and Branscomb, 1993 and 1994) rather than economics, although evaluation can be largely reinterpreted in the economic terms outlined above.

There is an "insurance" argument for specific technology programmes in terms of the need to have technologies in place if and when they will be needed. This is, of course, the major justification for defence R&D, including post-cold war programmes, but the argument has also been used to justify civil programmes. In the energy field, it has been a justification for programmes in renewable energy (*e.g.* solar voltaics) which cannot be justified in terms of current energy prices. One extension of this argument covers some new environment-related technologies, especially those concerned with threats of global climate change (Heaton *et al.,* 1992). Such programmes are necessarily difficult to evaluate.

A more general justification for national technology programmes has been to respond to other countries' programmes – the "level playing field". IT programmes in the United Kingdom (Alvey) and the United States (SemaTech) were conceived partly in these terms. EUREKA could be another example. These programmes are equally difficult to evaluate.

Human resource development has been a specific objective in a few programmes (Alvey); usually, this translates into promoting the movement of S&T personnel between academic and market-oriented occupations (NAS, NAE, IOM, 1992).

Chapter 2

Taxonomies/typologies of national programmes

Introduction

Chapter 1 above presented the available national data (as submitted to the OECD) on overall allocations of government and industrial R&D in relation to industry. This Chapter is concerned with more or less discrete technology programmes. In no sense is this an exhaustive review, and the notion of "national technology programmes" used is fairly broad, although the emphasis is on programmes that have been or could be evaluated in relation to economic and technology objectives.

It bears repeating that the range of data on specific programmes at present available represents only a small part of total national efforts with regard to industrial R&D. In fact, Tables 2 and 3 suggest that the identifiable DISP programmes may represent no more than 10 per cent of total direct OECD funding of enterprise R&D. Most of the government support unaccounted for seems to be through government procurement – which, from the point of view of "subsidies" to industry, should not be included because it is in support of wider government objectives (defence, social, environmental).

National programme objectives

Chapter 1 identified the various justifications for government intervention. These are reflected in the varying objectives of national technology programmes, which may co-exist in the same programme (and perhaps even clash). An initial typology[8] could involve the following categories:

- support to R&D in general;
- support for specific technologies, and in particular "generic" or "enabling" technologies;
- support for technologies seen to be important for non-commercial, public reasons, such as defence, social infrastructure, public health, etc.;
- commercialisation of R&D which government has supported for other reasons, mainly defence, energy, space and public health; and
- wider diffusion of government-supported R&D, especially to/through SMEs and better use of national laboratories.

One study for Canada attempted to identify different implicit objectives in federal R&D expenditures in relation to the various justifications for national intervention (Hanel and Palda, 1992). It estimates the allocation of these expenditures to the natural sciences and engineering by different agencies, distinguishing between the various market failure justifications (inappropriability and minimum economic size (MES)) and those relating to "technology for government outputs". Results are shown for 1986-87 (as rough estimated shares) in Table 6. The purpose of the study was to examine the extent to which

Table 6. **Canadian federal expenditure on R&D in the natural sciences and engineering, fiscal year 1986-87**

Percentage of total

Millions of Canadian dollars	Market failure		Technology for govt. outputs	Other [2]
	Inappropriability	MES [1]		
National research council 415	50	30	10	10
Agriculture Canada 372	66	34		
Energy, mines, resources 264	70			30
Natural science and engineering research council 251	84			16
National defence 220			100	
Regional industrial expansion 186	50			50
Medical research council 145	90		10	
Fisheries and oceans 128	71			29
Atomic Energy Canada limited 126	50			50
Environment 63			100	
Communications 63			100	
Total: C$ 2 234				

1. Minimum economic size.
2. Research on behalf of industry or subsidy to industry without apparent market failure or public goods justification.
Source: Hanel and Palda, 1992.

government support for enterprise sector R&D was based on market failure and technology for government outputs. The authors wrote of the results:

"The impressionistic tally, based on our interpretation of various departmental reports and federal statistics, is deliberately conservative in its estimates. That is, it probably assigns too much...expenditure to the two categories of market failure remedy and technology for government outputs. Of the (US$2.2 billion aggregate total)..., approximately two-thirds could be claimed to go toward the remedy of market failure. Of this, US$1.2 billion or 83 per cent, could be viewed as going toward the alleviation of inappropriability and the rest... US$250 million to offset the consequences of too large MES. Eighteen per cent, or about US$400 million would seem to fall under... technology for government outputs, such as defence technology or atmospheric research. The rest, about US$350 million or 16 per cent..., appears to be spent either in support of the private sector with little market failure justification, or to sustain bureau objectives. We repeat that this is likely a minimum estimate."

One example of a hierarchy of multiple objectives (technological, structural, strategic) in a single programme is the UK Alvey IT programme (see Chapter 4 below for its evaluation).

Ergas (1987) suggests a basic classification which distinguishes between technology policies that are "mission-oriented" (notably the United States, France and the United Kingdom) and those that are "diffusion-oriented" (e.g. Germany, Sweden and Switzerland). French innovation policies are discussed in OECD (1986). For the former, technology policies are primarily concerned with achieving specified public goals (e.g. in defence, industry, energy and public health). In the latter category, they are primarily about the provision of "public goods". Japan shows characteristics of both types of policy.

Pre-competitive and near-market research

Much of the interest in national technology programmes is due to their effects on competition, both within countries and, especially, internationally. Government support can represent an implicit or explicit subsidy to particular competitors. On the other hand, it is generally recognised that: i) the social returns to R&D expenditures are great; and ii) governments have legitimate public goods objectives driving their promotion of R&D. The competition policy problem is thus to determine what is acceptable.

One typology focus could be on the spectrum from basic research through development and demonstration to diffusion of new technologies. Another could be along the road from public goods to proprietary technology. In a simple view of technology development and diffusion, these two spectra would largely coincide with the application of basic research to the production of public goods, and with the appropriation of most near-market research. Thus, a distinction could be made between pre-competitive research (towards the basic end of the spectrum and leading to public information) and near-market research (which would be primarily proprietary).[9]

In the real world, however, the two blend, a fact reflected in national technology programmes. While one can identify steps along the first spectrum, the innovation process is not linear and may involve a complex interaction between the steps. As to the other spectrum, for some technologies more or less basic research is appropriable, while in others near-market research is not appropriable. At the two extremes, for reasons of national competitiveness, governments may seek to promote more basic research through encouraging appropriation of research results (*e.g.* US moves to patent human genome research) or, alternatively, to promote near-market research whose results are retained in the public domain (*e.g.* some environmental R&D). The result is that many programmes have multiple, even conflicting, objectives. This may especially be a problem for generic technologies, spin-off programmes and environmental programmes.

There are no general overall data available to allow a judgement on just how much identifiable programmes have supported different types of R&D along the two spectra. This report, with its focus on specific evaluated programmes, necessarily excludes most basic research and "very-near-market" R&D.

Stokes (1993) proposes a somewhat different typology of objectives, in which the key distinction is that between "understanding" and "use". There are two spectra: one concerns the extent to which R&D is sponsored in order to promote understanding of basic science, while the other concerns the extent to which it is motivated to find practical uses. Schematically, the spectra produce four quadrants (Table 7). Quadrants I and IV are areas where public funding of R&D is primarily motivated by the "understanding" objective. They may pose policy issues, but these are not about innovation policy. The difficult quadrants, from a policy point of view, are III – exclusively use-oriented R&D – and, especially, II – "strategic research" (the Pasteur quadrant) – where R&D is sponsored and motivated by concerns about promoting both understanding of basic science and its practical use. Stokes argues that existing statistics (including those from OECD) blur this understanding/use distinction, and thus, fail to identify the Pasteur quadrant.

From an international competition point of view, the EC has developed a basic distinction between:

   i) fundamental research: "an enlargement of general scientific and technical knowledge not linked to industrial or commercial objectives";

Table 7. **Research objectives**

| | | Is research oriented toward: applied use? | |
		No	Yes
Basic understanding?	Yes	I Pure basic research	II Strategic research
	No	IV	III Purely applied research

Source: Stokes, 1993.

28

ii) basic industrial research: "original theoretical and experimental work whose objective is to achieve new or better understanding of the laws of science and engineering as they might eventually apply to an industrial sector or the activities of a particular undertaking'';

iii) applied research and development: "the former covers investigation or experimental work based on the results of basic industrial research to acquire new knowledge to facilitate the attainment of specific practical objectives such as the creation of new products, production processes or services. It could normally be said to end with the creation of a first prototype. Development is considered to cover work based on applied research aimed at establishing new or substantially-improved products, production processes or services up to but not including industrial application and commercial exploitation''.

The current GATT negotiations on subsidies ("the Dunkel text'') are largely based on these definitions. The following subsidies "shall be non-actionable:

a) assistance for research activities conducted by firms or by higher education or research establishments on a contract basis with firms if:
the assistance covers not more than 50 per cent of the costs of basic industrial research or 25 per cent of the costs of applied research;
and provided that such assistance is limited exclusively to:
  i) personnel costs (researchers, technicians and other supporting staff employed exclusively in the research activity);
  ii) the costs of instrument, equipment, land and buildings used exclusively and permanently (except when disposed of on a commercial basis) for the research activity;
  iii) consultancy and equivalent services used exclusively for the research activity, including bought-in research, technical knowledge, patents, etc.;
  iv) additional overhead costs incurred directly as a result of the research activity;
  v) other running costs (such as those of materials, supplies and the like), incurred directly as a result of the research activity'.

In the context of current trade negotiations, Tyson (1992, p. 204) has characterised the basic distinctions above as "alarmingly vague''. She continues: "This language, which reflects an uneasy compromise between nations with different philosophical views, reveals that no one really knows what constitutes a pre-competitive applied research program. Many scientists and engineers believe that precise distinctions between basic, pre-competitive, and applied research cannot be made.''

Nevertheless, because of the need to justify programmes and associated evaluation requirements, there is policy interest in retaining a distinction between pre-competitive and near-market R&D. This is especially important for international programmes. Some are clearly labelled as pre-competitive (*e.g.* most EC programmes). In this context, the EC ESPRIT can be contrasted with the wider European EUREKA programme, which is clearly near-market. However, the distinction is not straightforward and there have been major overlaps (OECD, 1989*b*, p. 135).

Whether R&D can be counted as pre-competitive depends greatly on the structure of national innovation systems and on how governments manage their involvement. It is argued, for example, that there is a basic contrast between the US and Japanese systems (National Research Council, 1990). In the latter, the importance of research consortia, managed by a group of enterprises but with government sponsorship and university involvement, blurs the basic distinction (see for example Ergas, 1987, p. 221).

More generally, Callon et al. (1991 and 1992) have proposed a schema and framework of analysis for a "Techno-Economic Network" (TEN), which can be used to identify and evaluate a government role. This is represented in Table 8, while Table 9 simplifies and expands the analysis into an evaluation tool.

The analysis is particularly relevant to government technological programmes with broad and multiple objectives because it emphasises the links within the range of policies of the TEN. In the papers by Callon et al., the analysis is developed in relation to the activities of the Agence française pour la maîtrise de l'énergie (AFME). The overall (implicit) objective of the AFME is to develop "complete", "convergent" and "flexible" TENs in the energy sector which are responsive to overall government energy priorities. However, the TEN analysis would still be appropriate for government programmes with a more specific focus, by emphasising the importance of interaction throughout the entire TEN.

In their analysis of the impact of EC programmes on S&T in France, the same research group have identified the promotion of "basic technological research" (recherche technologique de base – RTB) as an important objective of EC programmes (Laredo and Callon, 1990, p. 166). Such efforts are seen as pre-competitive in the sense that they are "not oriented directly towards pilot production, prototypes, norms or

Table 8.   **The Techno-Economic Network**

Scientists/ researchers		Technologists/ engineers		Users/ buyers
Actors		Transfer apparatus	Companies – distribution	
SCIENCE (S)	*Transfer (ST)*	**TECHNICS (T)**	*Development (TM) commercialisation*	**MARKET (M)**
Intermediairies (examples)	Incorporates: Skills Experience Schemes Contracts	Models Patents Prototypes Software	Procedures Products	
Production of certified knowledge		Norms Rules of the art Trials		Diffusion of products

Source: Callon *et al.*, 1991 and 1992.

Table 9. **The Techno-Economic Network as an evaluation tool**

| | Breakthrough | Continuity | |
		Structuring actions	One-off actions
S			
ST			
T			
TM			
M			

Source: Callon *et al.*, 1991 and 1992.

patents''. Yet the promotion is technological in the sense that it is "oriented to industry and the technical competences required by firms''.

The authors point to the growing importance of large-scale computer modelling in EC-financed RTB – which is, in part, a substitute for specific experimentation, and which (consequently) yields general technological conclusions (that avoid some of the appropriability problems).

The authors claim that this development of RTB "calls in question the traditional classifications along the spectrum from theoretical knowledge to practical development problems''. Importantly, they claim that the EC programmes have promoted shifts in traditional patterns of relationships within French TENs.

In some national technology programmes, a sequence of phases is identified in the programme preparation. These would typically be cases where the ultimate programme objective is national success for a targeted product or process, but which start with pre-competitive R&D. Typically also, these are programmes for which the ultimate costs to governments are foreseen as large. The programmes reviewed in the Brookings study reported by Cohen and Noll (1991) are important (although complex) examples. However, there are smaller-scale examples, many involving risks. Such phased programmes greatly complicate the assessment of impacts.

Types of intervention instruments

While it is possible to distinguish broad types of intervention instruments – fiscal incentives, loans, grants, subsidies for R&D personnel, government procurement, government equity investment, finance for government-owned research institutions – a number of programmes involve a mix of instruments.

For some purposes, it is useful to distinguish direct instruments (grants, loans, equity) from indirect instruments (fiscal incentives and R&D personnel subsidies). Government procurement is difficult to classify. The direct/indirect distinction should be seen as a continuum. All the instruments are employed by governments in the innovation process, but for data and evaluation reasons this report is primarily concerned with fiscal incentives (indirect) and loans and grants (direct).

A related distinction applies to the specificity of technological objectives. Most technology-specific ("targeted") programmes involve direct instruments, while most indirect programmes are non-specific. However, the match is not inevitable – for example, fiscal incentives can be designed to target specific technologies.

Only a few Member countries have attempted estimates of both direct and indirect costs to government of R&D support to industry, and there are major problems of international comparability in the data. A Secretariat analysis in 1989 did suggest that the ratio of fiscal costs to direct R&D support for industrial development is very high in some countries – 16.8:1 in the United States; 1.0:1 in Canada; 0.8:1 in Australia – but much lower – 0.2:1 in both France and Germany (OECD, 1989a, p. 52). However, the report doubted if these ratios indicated much more than considerable national differences. Moreover, they presumably do not include government R&D support for non-economic purposes, especially defence and public health in the case of the United States.

An alternative OECD estimate coming from the Industry Committee work on "Subsidies and Structural Adjustment" suggests a very different degree of relative importance (see OECD, 1990a, and Table 10 below). Fiscal instruments seem much less important in most countries, but this may be because they were under-recorded.

An alternative estimate for Canada (Hanel and Palda, 1992) suggests that the ratio of corporate investment tax credits claimed for R&D to federal R&D grants (in Canadian dollars) shifted from 0.37:1 in 1978-79 to 3.02:1 in 1987-88.[10]

The balance of fiscal to direct programmes partly reflects corporate structures and, more generally, the structure of the national "innovation system". In particular, it seems that in some countries, small innovative firms simply will not benefit from fiscal measures because they do not have sufficient declared profits to set against eventual R&D tax credits. Thus, in Australia, the important fiscal programme has, for administrative reasons, a threshold (minimum annual R&D expenditures of A$ 50 000) which would exclude most SMEs. However, this is complemented by a parallel grant/loan programme.

Fiscal measures

Fiscal measures raise considerable definition and analysis problems.[11] All OECD Member countries allow the deduction of current industrial R&D expenditures from current income (OECD, 1990a). The treatment of R&D capital expenditures varies. Some countries consider them as current expenditures. Some allow R&D expenditures to be carried forward, as they do capital expenditures; in certain cases (e.g. Australia), more than 100 per cent of R&D expenditures can be deducted from current income. Some countries allow special credits for incremental R&D programmes (e.g. the United States), for R&D employees or for SMEs. No easy overall assessments of coverage are possible, which greatly complicates the impact assessment problem.

Table 10. **Government policy instruments used to support industrial R&D: 1985-86**

Approximate share of 1985-86 expenditures

Percentage

	Tax concessions	Grants	Loans	Grants + loans
United States	65	35		
Canada[1]		100		
Japan[2]	35	25		
CEC[1]		100		
Denmark		80	20	
France	25	75		
Germany	10	90		
Greece		100		
Ireland		100		
Italy		10	90	
Netherlands		50	40	10
Portugal		100		
Spain		100		
United Kingdom		65		35
Austria	50			50
Finland	22.5	37.5	40	
Norway		100		
Sweden[3]		70	30	
Switzerland		100		
Australia	70	30		

1. Tax concessions are not included.
2. Apart from tax concessions and grants, there are equity capital of 2.5 per cent and consignment subsidies of 40 per cent. Consignment subsidies involve research commissioned by central government from private industry associations, groups of private firms and government laboratories in national co-operative projects such as the Large-Scale Projects, or the Fifth-Generation Computer Project.
3. Excluding technical R&D support appropriations which go to private industry, universities and government-backed institutions via the National Board of Technical Development, STU. Sweden also has a policy of guarantees which consists of 1 per cent of the expenditure.

Source: OECD, 1990. Loans are at face value, *i.e.* gross government budget expenditure. Note that for Germany, the inclusion of data on support to industrial R&D by sub-central authorities may influence comparability with other countries.

Hanel and Palda (1992, Table 3) have attempted to rank important countries by the generosity of their R&D fiscal incentives using "B-indexes", which they define as "the after-tax cost of US$1 of R&D expenditure, divided by one minus the tax rate, or ATC/(1 – tax rate). The lower it is, the more hospitable the tax climate is to R&D outlays". The 1989 ranking for ten countries was (in declining order of generosity): Canada, Australia, Korea, France, United States, United Kingdom, Japan, Germany, Italy, Sweden.

For the period 1986-89, the DISP (OECD, 1992*b*) has 29 fiscal programmes in 14 Member countries for which R&D is either the principal objective or the principal economic cost. As many as ten further programmes in the same countries could be interpreted as being about technology promotion. The countries concerned (with number of programmes, where more than one) are: Australia; Austria – 3; Belgium – 4; Canada – 4; Denmark; Finland; France – 2; Germany – 3; Japan – 2; Portugal – 2; Spain; Switzerland; Turkey – 2; United States – 2.

Other sources suggest the existence – not necessarily in the same period as for the DISP – of significant fiscal concessions to R&D in other Member countries. The Bureau of Industry Economics (1989) reports and discusses programmes in the Netherlands, Sweden and the United Kingdom. That publication's main topic, however, concerns what is perhaps the most ambitious OECD programme: in 1985, the Australian Government implemented a tax concession at 150 per cent for R&D spending against corporate tax (see Box).

Fiscal programmes have much lower administrative costs than loans and grants. However, this is partly linked to programme targeting issues. Fiscal programmes have not generally been seen as a useful instrument to promote specific technology objectives. This partly reflects administrative policies and practices: tax departments are reluctant to accept specific objectives because these involve verification of conformity with difficult eligibility requirements, and any assessment of performance (even from public accountability concerns) is problematic.

Grants and loans

Grants and loans have been the principal policy instruments in specific technology programmes, and the DISP data suggests that their net cost to government (NCG) share, around 60 per cent in 1989, increased significantly over the 1986-89 period.

In general, it has seemed important for policy purposes that both grants and loans should be matched by contributions from programme participants. The policy concerns here have to do with additionality and, more generally, with motivating participants (and their parent institutions) to take the programmes seriously. There have also been competition policy concerns, both nationally and internationally, about identifying "acceptable" levels of subsidy: as outlined above, the EC has attempted to establish principles which have been brought into the current GATT negotiations. In most cases, the matching principle has been 50:50 (for the EC, 25:75 for applied research), but with higher government shares possible for particular cases (*e.g.* universities, SMEs). An OECD Secretariat attempt to summarise different Member countries' policies is outlined in Table 10. However, there is very little evidence available on the extent of this matching in practice, or on its effect on additionality.

The distinction between grants and loans is probably not very important in relation to most technology programmes. For the majority of loans, repayment is conditional on achieving profitable results, which would typically take several years.[12]

Public procurement and government equity participation

Public procurement is clearly a major instrument of support to industrial R&D, but it is very difficult to analyse. A rough calculation based on Tables 2 to 4 and the DISP data

Australia's tax concession scheme to promote R&D

In 1985, the Australian government implemented a tax concession against corporate tax of 150 per cent for R&D spending. The scheme aims to increase private sector spending on R&D, to promote collaboration between firms and public research institutions approved for the scheme, and to raise awareness about the importance of innovation. For administrative reasons, a minimum annual threshold of A$ 50 000 for R&D expenditures applies, thereby excluding most SMEs. However, the scheme is complemented by a parallel grant programme to assist companies unable to take advantage of the tax concession.

Initially, the tax concession was introduced at 150 per cent for a fixed period and was then to be reduced to 125 per cent. However, in 1992 the Government announced that the concession would be continued indefinitely at 150 per cent. The concession differs significantly from tax measures to assist R&D in other countries in that it applies to the total expenditure of firms, and not to the increase in R&D expenditure. This is justified in Australia's case on the basis of the still relatively low levels of Business Expenditure on R&D (BERD).

In 1987, provisions were introduced to enable to jointly register for the concession in order to undertake R&D projects that are too big or too risky for an individual company. This is commonly referred to as syndication. To date, 91 syndicates have been formally registered for the concession involving total expenditure of over A$ 1.3 billion. Syndication is in essence a form of venture capital finance for small to medium enterprises with carry-forward tax losses who are therefore unable to take advantage of the 150 per cent tax concession in their own right. The syndication arrangements provide critical mass finance for significant R&D projects that have reached a late stage in their development and which have good commercial prospects. A preliminary assessment of syndication indicates that it has been highly effective in terms of inducing new R&D and that for the firms involved it has substantially improved the scope for successful commercialisation.

The tax concession scheme also has special provisions for pilot plant, defined as an experimental model of R&D or commercial plant which is intended for use only in the R&D phase. Such plant is able to be claimed at the full rate of 150 per cent in equal instalments over the first three years in which the item of pilot plant is exclusively used for R&D. In 1992 a A$ 10 million limit on eligible pilot plant expenditure was removed, thereby expanding the scope for firms to undertake larger R&D projects.

At the time that the tax concession was introduced, Australia's BERD as a percentage of GDP was only 0.24 per cent – ranking 17th among OECD countries. In the period 1985-93, Australia's BERD approximately doubled in real terms.

At the time of the introduction of the tax incentive, Australia's corporate tax rate was 49 per cent. Thus the expenditure of a dollar on research resulted in an actual cost to a company of 26.5 cents, which was close to the assistance which a firm would normally receive through the parallel grant programme.

(continued on next page)

(continued)

However, there have been significant changes to Australia's business taxes since 1985. A dividend imputation system has been introduced and the corporate rate has recently been reduced to 33 per cent. As a result, the value of the incentive to firms has been reduced and a dollar spent on research now costs firms 50.5 cents. It is too soon to know whether, as a result of these changes, firms will reduce the rate of growth of their R&D.

Because of delays by companies in lodging claims to the tax concession, and because company tax returns can be revised after lodgement, the cost to revenue has had to be estimated. These estimates are further complicated by the divided imputation system, which is believed to erode part of the benefit and to partly reduce the cost to the Government. It is estimated that the cost to revenue of the tax concession was less than A$ 400 million in the financial year 1991-92.

In the Bureau of Industry Economies (BIE) 1993 evaluation of tax concession, the principal costs to Government are tax revenue foregone and administrative expenses. Costs to participating companies are incurred as a result of internal administration of R&D activities and compliance with the legislative requirements of the scheme (*i.e.* substantial). The BIE evaluation found that for a majority of scenarios the tax concession had a positive net welfare benefit; in other words, the social benefits of the concession (primarily induced R&D and spillover benefits) exceeded the social costs of the scheme (*i.e.* transfer payments and economic costs of funding the scheme). The BIE found that, for every dollar of tax revenue foregone, an additional A$ 0.60 to A$ 1.00 of R&D was induced.

In terms of the performance of the concession against its other sub-objectives, the BIE's overall conclusion was that its performance was at best indirect and in general uneven. There has been some additional collaborative R&D but the concession is only one of a number of factors influencing this activity. Because R&D costs are a significant proportion of total innovation costs, the concession is of indirect benefit in commercialising R&D results. The concession ranks in the middle of factors identified as important in determining the level of expenditure on R&D; other factors such as changing market opportunities and creating a competitive advantage were ranked by respondents as more important in the decision-making process.

The BIE also found that the concession played a role in changing corporate attitudes about R&D, however in relation to foreign-owned firms the BIE survey indicated that the concession had little effect on the transfer of R&D operations to Australia and that they are in general less responsive to the concession than Australian-owned firms. Small profitable companies were generally more responsive to the concession that other companies according to the BIE survey results.

Overall, while the BIE evaluation did not offer any quantitative estimates of the impact of the concession on the international competitiveness of Australian industry, the report concluded that the concession clearly contributes to increased innovativeness and is therefore likely to contribute to increased international competitiveness.

on identifiable (non-procurement) programmes suggests that public procurement must represent considerably more than half of aggregate government support to OECD industrial R&D.[13]

Much of this is concentrated in a few large countries and represents defence-related procurement (*e.g.* in the United States, France, the United Kingdom and perhaps Sweden), but analysis of the tables suggests that a significant part of it must consist of government appropriations which are not designated for defence purposes. Some procurement may represent energy appropriations, especially for nuclear energy (*e.g.* in Canada, France, Spain, the United Kingdom and, perhaps, Belgium). Some may concern emerging environmental policy concerns.

No useful data is available on government equity participation in relation to R&D. In the DISP, very few programmes for which government equity is the principal instrument have R&D as a principal objective. There are examples of important government equity investments, which certainly have explicit or implicit technology objectives, but these practically defy impact evaluation:

- It is difficult to identify the technology component (and especially the R&D).
- Much of the policy interest is not about nominal flows of capital, but rather about how the role of government in ownership and management affects corporate strategy and performance.
- There are formidable methodological difficulties in analysing the counterfactual issues.

Targeting specific objectives

National technology programmes vary considerably in the extent to which they target specific technologies or industries. Most of the targeted programmes are "direct" – as noted above, fiscal programmes are rarely used. Considerable interest revolves around the targeting of technologies judged to be "generic", "critical", "enabling" or "strategic". There is clear justification for government support on the grounds of market failure and non-appropriability.

No overall assessment of the extent or effectiveness of targeting is possible, because this depends as much on administrative practice as on stated objectives. The very notion of targeting is imprecise, as illustrated by the EUREKA programme; the general objectives are clearly targeted to the development of generic technologies and European competitiveness, but the choice and development of specific programmes are very much left to programme participants.

There are no general data on the share of specific programmes in total government R&D efforts (they are often included in wider programmes) and, as argued elsewhere, the importance of techno-economic networks suggests that the question of who actually receives government funding (or how it is received) – an administrative issue – may not be of much help in assessing its ultimate impacts. At the present stage of its development,

OECD's DISP cannot yet yield relevant results. However, the "crowding out" of other activities by a few large targeted activities is an important issue for some countries.

Spin-off/dual-use technology programmes

While most government R&D is not specifically directed to promoting industrial technology, much of it is potentially relevant. This mainly applies to R&D for defence and energy (especially in the United States), but it also concerns R&D in public health and agriculture. A growing policy concern is to maximise the use that can be made of this commercial R&D to enhance national competitiveness in industrial technologies. Several specific technology programmes are directed to this purpose; their impacts are reviewed in Chapter 4 below. More generally, government R&D laboratories are under increasing financial and policy pressure to find commercial outputs and justifications for their activities. The resulting programmes are not easy to analyse because they are not well documented, and so little evaluation experience has emerged. Most spin-off/dual-use programmes are not included in the DISP. Spin-offs from nuclear energy are extensively analysed in NEA (1993). US experience with specific programmes, especially for defence (DARPA) and energy (*e.g.* CRADA), are discussed in Alic *et al.* (1992), Branscomb (1993) and the NEA study. It is argued (NAS, NAE and IOM, 1992, and Tyson, 1992) that the situation is shifting from spin-offs to "spin-ons" (from commercial innovations to defence uses), and that dual-use technologies are now the important notion. This has important implications for the organisation of the programmes and the use of the national laboratories concerned (see Chapter 4 below).

Intellectual property rights (IPR)

Issues about the appropriation of technology are an important justification for government programmes, and the treatment of IPR is one indicator which could classify programmes. However, this is also an extremely difficult area in terms of evaluation. In many cases the stated objectives on appropriation lead to detailed negotiations between the programme partners, which cannot easily be captured in descriptions and eventual evaluations.

Methodologically, a distinction can be made between foreground and background IPRs. "Foreground" is what is generated in the programme; "background" is what a partner contributed. In both methodological (for evaluation purposes) and practical terms, these two categories must be treated differently.

OECD (1989*b*) considers different treatments in relation to several Member country IT programmes. The analysis illustrates the complexity and practical problems, but it does not address the obstacles to evaluation. Partly because the practical problems are complex, it is difficult to identify effective IPR arrangements in relation to other programmes.

Types of public management

Technology programmes can be distinguished in terms of government objectives for their management. The principal actors involved are the government (including national laboratories), the higher education sector (essentially universities) and various types of enterprise organisations (including industry research associations). The real difficulty is encountered in the important area of national research laboratories. Their role in relation to promoting industrial technology is not well documented and, in most cases, fairly marginal to their central mandate and organisation. This is largely because the primary mandate and justification of these institutions is not the promotion of industrial technology or competitiveness.

US analysis (NAS, NAE and IOM, 1992) makes a classification in terms of ownership and operation of the facilities/programmes, distinguishing between "government" and "contractors". Thus, it distinguishes between GOGO (government owned/government operated), GOCO (government owned/contractor operated) and COCO (contractor owned/contractor operated) programmes. In other OECD countries, this typology is perhaps less relevant. The ownership question may be less important than the operational arrangements, although ownership of national laboratories has recently become a policy issue in some countries, notably the United Kingdom. For the rather special case of nuclear energy, the shifting institutional arrangements are discussed in detail in the NEA (1993) report.

One large Canadian technology programme is the Industrial Research Assistance Programme (IRAP), which is part of that country's National Research Council. IRAP offers a variety of assistance options, which are tailored to the needs of the individual firm. Small and medium-sized firms (under 500 employees) can gain technical competence through a variety of sources: student assistance, consulting assistance and in-house projects (5 000 per year). The national element concerns itself with relatively large, technologically-significant industrial R&D projects involving collaboration with universities or government laboratories. Advisors from the National Research Council and other public sector science organisations are available to firms. About 400 projects per year are running; each lasts several years. The IRAP has an annual budget of C$ 90 million, which includes C$ 60 million in financial contributions to firms. The IRAP organisation is complex, involving administration of the different parts and co-ordination between firms and experts. IRAP is perceived to be a central link in a national technology network made up of public and private sector laboratories, universities, technical consultants, industry associations, foreign technology sources and public S&T policy-makers.

The public management issue is closely linked to that of targeting. A basic contrast has been suggested between the style of management of, for example, the EC programmes (top-down) and those of EUREKA (bottom-up). In the EC case, each programme needs advance approval that the R&D will conform to programme objectives. In the EUREKA case, potential collaborators determine a common R&D area of interest, which then (if approved) falls under a general umbrella. The Alvey Programme combined the two styles. It can be argued that bottom-up R&D collaborations are more likely to be commercially successful and durable. On the other hand, they are less likely to fulfil market failure criteria for justification.

Promoting innovation systems and networking

The notion of a techno-economic network has been developed by Callon *et al.* (1992) – see Tables 6 and 7. While the authors would argue that it has general relevance to the technological innovation and diffusion process (and to government intervention), it also has special relevance to the analysis of national innovation systems and technological diffusion.

Technology diffusion and the promotion of networks need a framework for analysis which links market-related activities with "upstream" science and technology activities. To a large extent, this is a positive proposition: it is impossible to make sense of the multiplicity and complexity of networking relationships without reference to an overall framework (the TEN) which links science, technology and the market. Moreover, empirical analysis of French AFME energy programmes confirms that the "linear" model is inappropriate.

What are legitimate/acceptable diffusion/networking objectives? Callon *et al.* distinguish "N2", the desirable TEN, from "N1", the actual TEN; government programme objectives should promote the progressive alignment of N1 and N2.

University-industry links form part of these TEN, and have been promoted in various government programmes. In value terms, they represent a very small portion of government efforts to promote industrial technology, and they are not generally included in the DISP. They are inevitably very diffuse and difficult to evaluate. One attempt to present and analyse the issues is contained in the Bureau of Industry Economics (1991) evaluation of the Australian National Teaching Company Scheme, which also draws on earlier OECD work and includes a description of comparable programmes in other OECD countries (Alic *et al.,* 1992; OTA, 1991).

The Directorate for Science, Technology and Industry has reviewed technology and competitiveness in relation to SMEs (OECD, 1993), and the report includes considerable discussion of government policies and programmes. Table 9 lists some government programmes active in the 1986-89 period, extracted from the DISP. However, it illustrates the multiplicity and heterogeneity of programmes to support SMEs – and, therefore, the problems of their evaluation. Conclusions are summarised in Chapter 4 below.

A few programmes have been formally evaluated; these are outlined here and discussed further in Chapter 4. The UK Department of Trade and Industry (DTI) launched in October 1986 the VANGUARD Awareness Initiative with the overall aim of raising awareness, mainly in the business community, of the benefits to be achieved by adopting electronic means of communicating between trading partners. Some 900 companies received introductory consultancy. In the second phase, a series of reports, teaching materials and a journal were commissioned. The initiative cost £3.5 million, which was paid by DTI and five sponsor firms.

The German BMFT (Federal Ministry for Research and Technology) provided DM 326 million to subsidise the application of computer-aided design and manufacture as part of its Production Technology Programme (1984-86). The action was aimed particularly at small and medium-sized firms. These enterprises were supported in development work for CAD/CAM implementation, receiving staff costs, hardware/software costs, and support for external contracts in consultancy, R&D and training, at 40 per cent of overall final cost. The scheme was an "indirect-specific" measure, which means that project application, acceptance and administration are simple and do not depend on the degree of project development, novelty or market potential.

One programme in the United Kingdom, SMART (Small Firms Merit Award for Research and Technology), aimed to stimulate innovative projects in start-ups and other firms with less than 200 employees. SMART set up a highly competitive and prestigious award scheme for innovation projects. The pilot took place in 1986 with 20 Stage I awards of up to 75 per cent of project costs, to a maximum of £37 500. The scheme has grown, with 140 Stage I awards in 1987 and 180 in 1990. In 1989 the firm size was limited to 49 employees. Stage II awards involve 50 per cent of project costs up to £50 000. Firms are picked from regional competitors and the awards administered by regional offices of the UK DTI. The criteria for choosing include the quality and novelty of the product, the need for public support, the quality of the personnel and the potential commercial benefit to the United Kingdom of the proposed product. Another objective of the scheme was to attract private funding to high-risk technology projects and to encourage firms to market ideas through the high profile of the scheme and the publicity surrounding the competitors.

National versus international programmes

Technology programmes can be classified by their national orientation, reflecting the trade-off between promoting national competitiveness and obtaining access to, and economies of scale in, international programmes. Clearly, the trade-off is more difficult for smaller countries and varies with the type of technology involved.

In some areas of technology, there is clear public interest in international collaboration. In economic terms, these would be activities with substantial indivisibilities and economies of scale, or substantial risks and international externalities (perhaps the best example of which is environmentally-"clean" technology). A cross-cutting typology is possible here with the analysis of pre-competitive and near-market programmes. Pre-competitive technology programmes have more easily found justification for international co-operation than near-market programmes. However, it is very difficult to identify this distinction in relation to the expressed objectives of national programmes and national competitiveness. Distributional criteria are an immediate objective in some cases.

Most countries emphasise national competitiveness objectives in the majority of their programmes. In the larger countries, most programmes restrict participation to "national" organisations, especially in the case of enterprises. Moreover, in some cases (*e.g.* Australia), the criteria for access stipulate that the programme should enhance national competitiveness. To some extent, this becomes a question of the location of the R&D involved. However, there follows the major problem of globalisation of technology development and diffusion, and the status of multinational enterprises.

No useful aggregate data are available on international programmes. There is considerable literature on EC programmes, but these are a very special case, and it is difficult to relate them to analysis of other national involvement in international programmes. EUREKA programmes can be outlined, but because of the decentralised nature of EUREKA funding, no aggregate assessment of their importance is possible. International collaborative aspects of programmes are not identified in the DISP.

Smaller or more technologically-backward countries have a special interest in international R&D collaboration, for reasons of indivisibility. However, there is little empirical evidence to measure the extent to which their programmes are more "international", or their style of management different.

International collaboration may seem justified in technology areas for which there will be a clear need for international standards when the technology in question becomes competitive.

A more general objective is to promote international collaboration between R&D institutions. The criteria for success here could simply be the number of collaborators networking. However, questions remain as to the quality and (especially) durability of the resulting networks. Direct surveying of participating institutions has also been suggested. Cross-country bibliometric indicators could prove useful in this regard, as could cross-country patenting (EC, 1991).

Chapter 3

Evaluation methodologies and problems

Introduction

There is now considerable activity in the area of R&D programme evaluation in the OECD Member countries, including work on methodological issues. Available published evaluations reflect a wide variety of approaches to match different institutional and methodological concerns. At the same time, there is considerable agreement that evaluation has lagged behind the development of official R&D programmes.

A major part of the current evaluation problem concerns the national technology programmes which are the focus of this report, and the evolving notions of technology innovation and diffusion discussed in Chapter 1. Until now, however, evaluation has dealt primarily with public accountability (both financial and administrative) and programme management, including the planning of new projects (Bureau of Industry Economics, 1992; Ormala, 1989). Much of it has concerned R&D which is outside the notions of technology programmes developed here (Chapter 2). This further complicates the evaluation task and increases the need for methodology.

Objectives in evaluation

In the process of establishing the policies for most national programmes which are at all specific, it is necessary to stipulate some sort of evaluation. However, much of what results is about how the programme was actually conducted and public money spent, about how much the programmes related to their stated objectives, and about feeding the answers back into the policy process.

Importantly, the public accountability and project management objectives require most of the evaluation to be conducted during or immediately after the programme life (*i.e.* in "real time"). This has led to the development of intermediate programme indicators – proxies for programme outputs – and much discussion of the appropriateness of indicators generally, especially in the context of EC programmes. Of major interest in this regard are the activities and publications of the EC's Monitor/Spear programme, reviewed in Bobe (1991) and Olds (1992).

There is another body of research literature which is concerned with wider issues than accountability and management; this analysis, which is more immediately relevant to the technology and economic impacts issues outlined above, tends to be *ex post,* in that it is performed several years (in some cases a decade or more) after completion of the programme.

Whatever the immediate source of data on impacts, the ultimate source is the official programme evaluations, which quickly raises the problem of identifying and assessing longer-term impacts. Many years may pass after the completion of an R&D programme before innovation is realised or (more generally) economic impacts recognised. Thus, intermediate indicators are needed. However, it should be noted that these longer-term impacts have not seemed central to most programme evaluation and that, given the non-linear nature of the innovation process, they are not easy to identify in advance.

The problem of longer-term impacts is part of the larger evaluation problem of causality. There are two relevant questions:
- What would have happened without the government intervention?
- To what extent was the actual outcome of the programme – the impacts – the result of the programme?

The first question is particularly relevant to fiscal R&D programmes, and has been addressed directly in a few evaluations (Bureau of Industry Economics, 1989 for Australia; Cordes, 1989 for the United States). However, it is also relevant to direct government finance. Would the participants have performed the R&D in any case? How did the existence of the programme affect the outcome? Did it speed up or slow down the R&D, or entail more participants? It is particularly relevant to programmes such as the UK Alvey programming for IT, for which a central objective was a better "networking" of research initially judged to be too fragmented.

A related issue is additionality. Did the existence of the programme lead to additional associated R&D/innovation activities which were not financed by the programme and which would not otherwise have occurred? This can be linked to the desirability of raising R&D expenditures in the aggregate, and is discussed in the Australian Bureau of Industry Economics evaluations. It has also been addressed directly through surveys in some evaluations of grant and loan programmes which require matching (generally 50:50) participant finance. However, survey evidence on these counterfactual questions may be especially unreliable.

Additionality poses particular problems for some international programmes – to what extent did international government finance simply replace national government finance, or distort national priorities? This question has been covered in the evaluation of some EC programmes, where issues of subsidiarity are relevant to policy (Olds, 1992).

The second causality question, the extent to which programme outcomes resulted from the programme, is a difficult one, mainly because of the "non-linearity" problem and uncertainty in the innovation process. For example, in his evaluation of several EC BRITE programmes, Toulemonde found that, during the course of some of them, it became apparent that there could be other commercial applications of the research apart from those specifically identified as programme objectives (see Table 11 below, and Bureau of Industry Economics, 1992).

More generally, programmes which run over several years are subject to exogenous events which greatly affect programme performance and outcomes. Even with an essentially pre-commercial programme, Alvey, it was found that the continuing restructuring of the UK IT sector affected the participation of UK firms (Alvey, 1991). With near-market programmes, the problems posed by exogenous events are clearly greater (see Chapter 4 below).

The "institutionalisation" of the evaluation process

Much of the discussion about evaluation concerns the "institutionalisation" of efficient processes. The key interlocking factors here are:

- the need to generate reliable data and co-operation from programme participants;
- the costs of data creation;

Table 11. **Economic evaluation experience with the BRITE Programme**

BRITE contract No.	1045	1391	1354a	1354b	1079	1289	Average
Paternity[1] (%)							
BRITE/research	100	95	50	10	50	40	57
Research/result	100	100	100	20	100	90	85
Risks[2] (%)							
Technical					10		2
Socio-economic	40			50		50	23
Supplementary R&D cost[3]	2	0	4	3	3	0	2.0
Distance from market[4]	2	2	4	5	1	3	2.8
Pre-competitiveness[5]	1	0	0	4	30	1.3	
Market[6]							
Immediate	1 000	> 1	50	50	19 020		
Potential	10 000	> 1			5		
Longer-term	2 500				50 000		

1. Share in the decision to launch the research attributable to the programme, share in scientific results attributed to the research, share in the potential economic impact attributable to the contract.
2. Technical risk = probability that the R&D fails for technical reasons. Socio-economic risk = probability that the development decision is not taken inspite of technical success.
3. Ratio of complementary R&D to programme research costs.
4. Number of successive intervening actors before first marketing stage.
5. Number of competitors who could profit from the research before it reaches the first market.
6. Expected annual (EU) turnover (ECU million) for contractor.
Source: Adapted from Toulemonde, 1990, p. 44. For further explanation, see text and reference.

- the need for independent assessment; and
- the need to feed assessment efficiently back into programme development and policy.

While these questions are not central to the evaluation of technology and economic impacts (their primary concern is with public accountability and programme management), they are indirectly and, indeed, importantly related. A better institutionalisation of the evaluation process could lead to a better selection of programmes – and to a better and more independent source of evaluation data on a wider variety of programmes.

In fact, one of the major problems here concerns the independence of the evaluations, and the transparency and credibility of the results. This is particularly relevant to the use of surveys, reviewed below. Much of the evaluation literature is concerned with setting up systems which are both institutionalised and, at the same time, independent and transparent. For the EC, Chabbal (1987) has proposed complex arrangements that would integrate the different agents in R&D programmes and put them under the ultimate supervision of a *garant*.

In the case of the UK Alvey programme, the hierarchical structure of programme objectives that had been established from the beginning allowed a definition of, and mechanisms for, evaluation which were built into the programme's organisation and financing.

This was also the case with Australian programmes. From the start the independent Bureau of Industry Economics was brought in for the evaluation. The BIE's experience has already led to the development of six key steps to be applied to each of its evaluations:

- *i)* Terms of reference are developed in consultation with programme managers.
- *ii)* Managers are required to finance some of the evaluation costs.
- *iii)* Programme administrators join the review team.
- *iv)* There are drafts to further the consultation process before the review is completed.
- *v)* Evaluation results are published.
- *vi)* There is co-operation and feedback for policy review and formulation.

In addition, there was more general public accountability evaluation (Auditor-General, 1989).

At the same time, there can be problems of independence and transparency in institutionalised evaluation, especially in relation to economic issues and technology innovation and diffusion. Programme objectives tend to be general, and where they are specific they are not always easy to evaluate in relation to outcomes. Some programmes involve ill-articulated distributional criteria. Most institutionalised evaluations do not seek to go much beyond the established objectives; this has led to an increased interest in independent evaluation (see NAS, NAE and IOM, 1992, regarding the need in the United States for ''arm's-length'' assessment for future programmes).

Very little data is available on the costs of data creation and evaluation. ''Internalising'' the evaluation within the programme process should lead to cost reductions in both domains (by creating accepted mechanisms). In relation to EC programmes, Chabbal (1987) has suggested that in an institutionalised process which nevertheless makes use of external consultants, "evaluation costs will... vary greatly from one programme to another and will represent between 0.25 per cent and 1.0 per cent of the total cost of a programme. This should be compared with the figure of 4.0 per cent currently regarded as the average cost of programme management". Chabbal breaks down the costs as follows (in 1987 prices):

    i) evaluation committee – ECU 100 000;
    ii) external consultancy interview – ECU 30 000 - ECU 100 000;
    iii) post-evaluation – ECU 50 000 - ECU 150 000.

The ECU 180 000 - ECU 350 000 total is an indication that the institutionalised process should apply to programmes of upwards of ECU 25 million. Clearly some grouping of individual programmes would be required, which could have implications for the evaluation process and for the impacts analysed.

Chabbal compares this with a cost, for a similarly institutionalised process but for fully completed programmes, in the French AFME (*Agence française pour la maîtrise de l'énergie*) of about ECU 100 000 (1987 prices) for studies covering "narrow sectors".

Toulemonde (1990) has suggested that the costs of his proposed institutionalised but "directed" economic appraisals could be between ECU 2 000 and ECU 3 000 for an outside expert – much lower than the Chabbal estimates.

These data on evaluation programme costs raise several issues. First, at the present level of costs, detailed evaluation of economic impacts is inhibited. What would be an acceptable cost level for more adequate evaluation?

Secondly, while institutionalising the process and costs may lead to savings, *internalising* the costs may inhibit the willingness of participants to co-operate in evaluation (and perhaps even discourage them from participating altogether).

On the other hand, relatively high costs may bias the evaluation process towards large programmes (or towards the aggregation of programmes, with a corresponding lack of specificity) and aggravate the problems of non-co-operation and non-response. There is also difficulty in making the transition to more institutionalised evaluation. In the present situation, programmes that are more intensively investigated may receive more critical attention than those that are not. This may introduce bias into overall assessments.

However, from an – especially economic – impacts point of view, it is difficult to know in advance what data will be required, or predict what the precise outcomes of an R&D programme will be. It is important once again to recognise that the innovation process is not linear.

To the extent that the evaluation objective is economic (competitiveness) and the programme is near-market, there are confidentiality problems with regard to the data required. In an institutionalised transparent process, respondents may be unwilling to indicate *ex ante* their current commercial expectations, and the programme sponsors may be unwilling to insist. Alternatively, there may be complicity in generating unrealistic estimates of programme benefits.

Economic evaluation of national technology programmes

There is a great deal of literature on the economic evaluation of returns to R&D expenditures, which has been extensively reviewed (see for example, Capron, 1992 and 1993; Mairesse and Sassenou, 1991*a* and *b*; Mohnen, 1991). While the results are generally positive (if inconclusive), there are important methodological problems. The general difficulties concern the quantification of both technology inputs and economic outputs and the links between the two. On the input side, there is a major problem about distinguishing R&D from other (especially technology) inputs. On the output side, the problem is discerning the extent to which the benefits are located within a specific sector (or programme) and how far they can be traced economy-wide (the spillover problem). Conceptually, studies can be classified according to their focus on the relationships at micro- (including programme-based), mesa- (sectorial) and macroeconomic level. Here, there is a trade-off between what can be identified and broader impacts (including spillovers) that are very difficult to interpret.

More importantly, there has been little attempt to use econometric or other model-ling techniques directly to assess the role of government support (Alic *et al.,* 1992, Capron, 1992 and 1993). Most of the available studies have government R&D as only one variable in a wider analysis. Very broadly, the studies address one of two approaches (Capron, 1992, p. 144):

> `` *i)* the productivity approach which measures the respective effects of privately-funded and publicly-funded R&D expenses on the growth rate of output, so giving an evaluation of the output elasticity of public R&D or of the rate of return on public R&D;
>
> *ii)* the investment approach which measures to what extent public R&D alloca-tions influence privately-funded R&D expenditures, the idea being to look at whether, by doing its own R&D and funding private R&D, a government affects (positively, negatively, or not at all) the privately-funded R&D and the magnitude of the effect.''

On the productivity approach, Capron's review points to methodological difficulties and inconclusive results. Part of the problem obviously comes from the different objec-tives and modalities of government R&D (especially, public goods and basic research) and, in industry-wide analysis, the importance of sectors (``outliers''), such as defence, where productivity/output increases are imperfectly measured. (Most of the studies con-cern the United States.) More generally, productivity returns to intangible investments such as R&D have proved very difficult to capture econometrically: they tend to remain residuals. The studies suggest that government R&D is far less productive than private R&D, and cannot conclusively be shown to be positive in the aggregate, ``may be largely unproductive'' says Capron (1992, p. 153), but that there are wide variations between sectors.

On the investment approach (how far government R&D promotes additional private R&D), the econometric research seems to be on safer empirical ground, but the results are still inconclusive. There are massive differences in results between different studies. Again – and especially in the US studies – defence R&D seems to distort the overall results, probably because of the nature of the research. The effectiveness of government R&D in promoting private R&D may be linked to the size of the private firm or its existing "R&D intensity", but once again the evidence is conflicting. It has been argued (*e.g.* Lichtenberg, 1987) that the methodologies that yield positive results for the United States contain serious implicit upward biases. For one thing, it is difficult to disentangle government procurement from government R&D finance.

One cross-country analysis (Levy, 1990) found strongly conflicting results, but no satisfactory explanation: on balance, the impact of government R&D on private R&D was fairly positive (0.33), was strongly negative in the United Kingdom and the Netherlands, very positive in Japan, Sweden and Switzerland, and moderately positive in France, Germany, Italy and the United States. This result cannot easily be explained by defence R&D.

It should be emphasised that the inconclusiveness of the econometric studies using the investment approach does not imply that government R&D is ineffective. Some of the studies suggest a significant crowding-out of private R&D. Others suggest that public R&D promotes additional private R&D, although most indicate that the latter will be no more than US$0.25 per dollar of public R&D. However, the government financial intervention is itself additional in aggregate R&D terms, unless there is significant crowding-out. Even given administrative and deadweight costs of government intervention, the returns to the government investment may be very positive – but on this, in econometric terms, there is only the inconclusive evidence from the productivity approach.

It was noted in Chapter 1 that strategic R&D decisions typically take place in a context of oligopolistic international competition, in which governments have different objectives and are not always dominant players. This suggests that evaluation should make use of the games theory in economic analysis. Existing attempts to use this approach in the evaluation of government R&D impacts are reviewed by Capron (1992, Chapter 6) and Capron and Debande (1993). Capron concludes:

"The implementation of science and technology policy is, to a large extent, guided by strategic considerations. Technology is a non-price competitive weapon on which governments act by developing their science and technology policy. Not only technological rivalry between firms leads them to engage in a strategic race to innovate but also governments adopt a strategic behaviour in the design of their policies. In the past few years, some normative models of technology rivalry have been developed but, so far, this new theoretical modelling approach has not provided clear-cut prescriptions about the guidance of R&D policy. Besides, some more pragmatic studies which consider certain strategic issues show how difficult it is to implement an efficient R&D policy because of, among other things, the existence of agglomeration economies, the differences among industries, the outflow outside national borders of new knowledge, the specificities of the different types of R&D. As government actions in the field of science and technology are increasingly prompted by strategic issues, the evaluation of the economic impact of R&D policy should take this dimension into account. Future empirical investigations might consider models of competitive behaviour in oligopolistic markets."

Thus, econometric and games-theory analysis of the economic impacts of government support to R&D is problematic, although it provides a framework for further discussion and research. This explains the interest in formal evaluations of specific programmes.

In cost/benefit terms, the problems are largely about the evaluation of benefits, especially the longer-term benefits associated with innovation and externalities. However, there are also difficulties on the costs side; *i.e.* "opportunity costs" to governments, other programme participants and the national economy in conducting specific programmes. Thus, one Canadian study for the Economic Council (Tarasofsky, 1984) estimated that the total cost per dollar of subsidy paid, for loan/grant programmes assessed in the early 1980s, was around C\$ 1.81, with the following (average) breakdown:

- conception and administering the subsidy programme – C\$ 0.10;
- cost to firms applying for subsidies – C\$ 0.05;
- cost to taxpayers of tax compliance – C\$ 0.06;
- deadweight loss resulting from tax – C\$ 0.60.

For governments, the most important costs seem to be deadweight (those incurred by the economy when taxpayers rearrange their economic activities in response to a tax). The Canadian study estimate was "arbitrarily positioned within the range of various estimates" (Barbarie, 1990).

Australian analysis suggests that the administrative costs of government R&D programmes have been around 11 per cent for direct subsidy programmes, roughly comparable to the Canadian estimates, but only around 0.6 - 0.9 per cent for the fiscal programmes (Bureau of Industry Economics, 1989). Those lower costs notwithstanding, there may be a trade-off in programme benefits between more or less targeted objectives, and in their evaluation. More narrowly focused fiscal programmes would be possible but their administrative costs would rise, while direct programmes could be more broad-based with lower overhead administrative costs.

There are fungibility issues in the analysis of opportunity costs. To the extent that government funds are earmarked for R&D promotion, there is limited interest in analysing the deadweight costs. The more relevant questions concern alternative R&D uses for the same funds.

The opportunity costs to firms for participating in government R&D programmes have scarcely been assessed. In general, most evaluations assume that if firms participate, they do so for rational commercial reasons: opportunity costs can then be ignored. There is, of course, the question of how far firms were disappointed in the collaboration *vis-à-vis* their expectations.[14] Some evaluations have addressed this issue (see, for example, Alvey, 1991), which is complicated by the uncertainties and risks in the innovation process. The fact that firms were disappointed in their expectations is not, from a national economic point of view, conclusive evidence that the programmes were a mistake. In any case, it appears that the opportunity costs of government R&D programmes are significant, perhaps twice the nominal costs.

The evaluation problems are intractable for economic benefits, because these involve long time spans and externalities concerned with the innovation process. In fact, their long-term nature raises very important questions about which real discount rate (net of inflation) to use in evaluating future benefits. A "high" discount rate (say, 10 per cent) will disqualify most benefits occurring after 10 to 15 years. This would be a rate that corresponded to most commercial judgements. Even a "low" discount rate (say, 3 per cent – which would correspond to relatively optimistic judgements about world macroeconomic development) will disqualify most benefits after 25 years.

It is possible to argue for a low discount rate in the presence of social externalities or inter-generational benefits (*e.g.* environmental R&D, defence). Alternatively, and arguably more correctly from an economic viewpoint, an attempt can be made to place a "realistic" social value on the benefits, which may (or may not) be higher than expected market values. Either way, there are evaluation problems: a very low discount rate may distort (bias positively) government participation in projects alongside of collaborators using market rates, while there are credibility and methodological problems about assigning social values to long-term (and especially inter-generational) benefits.

On the whole, the published evaluations using formal cost/benefit analysis have used real discount rates at least as high as market real rates.[15] Thus, the evaluation performed by the Australian Bureau of Industry Economics (1992) for four CSIRO industrial research programmes uses a 10 per cent real rate, and the Brookings analysis of six "near-market" programmes uses a real rate of 7-10 per cent (Cohen and Noll, 1991). Sensitivity analysis suggested significantly higher benefit/cost ratios with lower rates.

Tyson has noted that the discount rate, when used to calculate the subsidy element in government loans, can become a potential source of system friction in international competition (1992, p. 283). In the Airbus argument between the United States and Europe, the United States contended that commercial market rates should be used, while Europe's view was that the appropriate rate should be the one at which governments can borrow.

Conventional cost/benefit analysis within a neo-classical economic framework will quickly prove inadequate when externalities come into play. These are linked to the causality questions outlined above: it needs to be shown that the externality benefits were the result of the programme and that they are different from (*i.e.* greater than) those that would have resulted from alternative uses of the same public funds. These are formidable evaluation constraints that are not generally addressed in most evaluation literature.

In practical evaluation terms, the problem is to judge which and how much of the eventual benefits should return to the government for its share of programme costs. As a rule of thumb, it is often assumed that for every dollar of research, there are 10 dollars of development and 100 dollars of commercialisation (Bureau of Industry Economics, 1992). However, governments may intervene at different stages in this non-linear process. In both the CSIRO and Brookings analyses, benefits were allocated as much as possible to total "programme" costs. This may bias the results upward, perhaps considerably, either because the final-stage commercialisation costs are difficult to estimate or because, as in some of the Brookings cases, they were hypothetical as the programmes were aborted or drastically reshaped (Cohen and Noll, 1991).

The economic evaluation problem is further complicated by the analysis of technology trajectories, innovation systems and the move away from neo-classical concepts towards new models of economic growth. These thrusts greatly strengthen the need for evaluation of externalities, spillovers and diffusion effects, even where those are not an original objective of the programme. Technology trajectories are explicitly considered in CSIRO prospective evaluation (Bureau of Industry Economics, 1992). However, most of the existing evaluations have "fudged" these economic issues. Externalities escape assessment; goals are expressed in technological terms, and results (what was achieved?) are viewed positively.

The *Bureau d'économie théorique et appliquée* at Strasbourg (BETA) has developed a methodology for analysing economic impacts of specific programmes, primarily those of the EC (BRITE/EURAM) and the European Space Agency (ESA); it has also been applied to Canadian space programmes (see Bach and Lambert, 1993; Bach *et al.,* 1992; BETA, 1988 and 1993). The methodology is summarised in Table 12, results for EC and ESA programmes in Tables 13 and 14 (see Chapter 4 and Conclusions below). The analysis seeks to quantify (value) the programme effects through detailed surveying of a representative sample of participants. Direct effects are those that come from meeting the narrowly defined objectives of the programme. They are valued in terms of sales or value added attributed to the EC programme by participants.

Indirect effects ("spin-offs") are benefits to participants (and, to some extent, their suppliers) beyond the narrowly defined programme objectives. They are classified in terms of four factors: technological, commercial, O&M and the work factor (see Table 12). For each type of effect, the quantification is in two stages: i) the share of the

Table 12. **BETA classification of effects**

Types of effect	Quantification
Direct effects	Sales/cost reduction
Indirect effects	
Technological	
Transfer of product	Sales/new research contracts
Transfer of process	Cost reduction/new research contracts
Transfer of services	Sales/new research contracts
Patents	Cost for establishing and holding the patent (proxy value)
Commercial	
Network effect	Sales/cost reduction/new research contract
O&M	
Project management	Cost reduction
Organisation	Cost reduction/sales/new research contracts
Method	Budget (proxy value)
	Cost reduction
Work factor	
Competence	Monetary equivalent of man-hours
Training	(proxy value)

Source: BETA, 1993.

52

Table 13.   **BETA/EURAM programmes: ratio of effects to EC funding**[1]

	January 1994 (est.)	January 1996 (projected)
Direct effects	10.5	13.3
Indirect effects	3.4	4.1
Shares in indirect effects (percentage of total)		
Technological		47.6
Commercial		10.3
Organisation and method		11.6
Competence and training		30.6

1.   Number of projects: 50. Number of participants (partners): 176. Number of measured economic effects: 611.
Source: Adapted from BETA, 1993 (p. 20). For explanation, see text and original reference.

Table 14.   **Indirect effects of space programmes**

	ESA 1980	ESA 1988	Canada 1989
Period covered	1964-82	1977-91	1979-93
Number of firms in panel	128	67	10
Total indirect effects (ECU mn)[1]	7 551	12 680	256
Among ESA contractors (ECU mn)[1]	6 023	9 214	189
Ratio effects/contracts	**> 2.9**	**> 3.2**	**> 3.5**
Nature of the effects (percentage of contractors' effects)			
Technological	25	43	40
Commercial	27	8	18
Organisation and methods	19	7	18
Work factor	29	41	24

1.   ECU 1986 for ESA, ECU 1989 for Canada.
Source: Bach and Lambert, 1993.

specific government programme in the total effects, assessed by BETA in discussion with programme participants (this can vary between 0 and 1); and ii) the contribution of each of the four factors to the total indirect effects (the shares must add up to 100 per cent). Bach *et al.* (1992, p. 188) argue that the results are necessarily minimum estimates of the effects because the assessment procedure is conservative, because participants may fail to recognise all the effects, and because effects are only introduced when they can be quantified. More generally, they do not include all the externalities/spillovers because they are based exclusively on the experience of programme participants.

The results of the various analyses employing this methodology to assess spin-offs are presented in Tables 13 and 14, and discussed in Chapter 4. The results are generally positive.

In both the CSIRO and Brookings evaluations, the formal cost/benefit analysis yielded significantly positive benefit-to-cost ratios on most assumptions, justifying *ex ante* the development of the programmes. In the CSIRO case, the ratios were around 2:0. However, in the Brookings cases, the simulated results deteriorated steadily as the programmes developed because (real) costs rose and technical/commercial outcomes became more problematic.

The CSIRO formal cost/benefit evaluation found that potential externalities and spillovers (demonstration effects) were not important, and that cost/benefit analysis was a very useful tool – particularly as a built-in safeguard against double-counting of benefits. It was also found that CSIRO's existing "priorities assessment framework" for *ex ante* evaluation procedures was logically compatible with cost/benefit analysis, and could be institutionally preferable in terms of information requirements and focusing programme discussion. In the case of a programme to develop industry standards and norms, it was found that "cost/efficiency" calculations were preferable to full cost/benefit analysis because values could not be assigned to the outputs.

Economic evaluation of impacts needs to encompass "sunk" costs. Some of the technology programmes specifically aim to use and diffuse the results of R&D which has been developed for non-economic objectives or that of programmes which have been aborted or have lost their original objectives. Here, there is an economic case for treating the historic costs as "sunk" and doing the evaluation in terms of the marginal costs related to the new/revised objectives which will, of course, produce much more favourable results for the programme. This approach could apply to commercial spin-offs from national laboratories or, more generally, from public health, agricultural or defence R&D. There has been very little formal economic evaluation of such programmes, although there is considerable documentation showing their importance (NEA, 1993; NAS, NAE and IOM, 1992).

Spin-offs raise important issues about the "rules of the game" and the "level playing field". To the extent that government finance for all research up to near-market and for non-commercial objectives can be considered as outside the evaluation, the assessment of "impacts" from specific further programmes may not represent the real costs to national economies. This takes policy analysis back into the very difficult area of justification for government support for basic and pre-competitive research – how far such research should be in the public domain, and the rules for international access.

Spin-off and dual-use programmes also pose counterfactual problems,[16] but perhaps the most difficult question in this area concerns the possibility of purchasing the outcome of the R&D programme from abroad rather than trying to perform it nationally. To what extent is it efficient or legitimate to be a "free-rider"? This is a general issue, but obviously more important for small countries. It is a major problem for large programmes with long-term technical and commercial uncertainties about outcomes. Greatly complicating matters are the associated problems of technology trajectories and commercial competition between a very small number of suppliers. For evaluation, there is an additional difficulty: most of the available evidence comes from interested parties and/or research personnel who are simply not in a position to make judgements about commercial outcomes (Toulemonde, 1990).

Other evaluation tools and practices

The discussion above establishes the need for intermediate programme indicators – mainly for basic and pre-competitive research, but also for near-market research. Most intermediate indicators are about networking, bibliometrics and intellectual property rights (essentially patents), and involve surveying of programme participants and, in some cases, control groups of non-participants. Of major interest in this regard are the activities and publications of the EC's MONITOR/SPEAR programme, reviewed in Bobe (1991) and Olds (1992).

One strand in the discussion concerns the quality of the research, for which there are well-established (if sometimes problematic) evaluation procedures involving peer groups and bibliometrics. However, it is widely accepted that research quality is not of primary relevance in assessing the impacts of national technology programmes (Barbarie, 1990), and that there is a need for changes in evaluation techniques (Krull et al., 1991).

Intermediate indicators require a reference framework. In their analysis of the impact of EC programmes in France, Laredo and Callon (1990) were surprised that norms and patents were not rated as important while publications and academic theses were assigned considerable importance. They explain their unexpected results in terms of the novel types of research and links promoted by the EC programmes. However, the conclusion here is that no simple standards of reference by which to judge official programmes are possible.

Callon et al. (1991 and 1992) emphasise that intermediate results are valuable in themselves, and not just as a proxy for final programme results. Importantly, they can trace the effects of a sequence of government actions at different points in a techno-economic network (TEN). Table 7 suggests a framework for such an analysis, and Callon et al. (1991 and 1992) illustrate the proposed technique in relation to two AFME programmes (on geothermal energy and the development of new heat exchangers).

Surveying of programme participants

Surveying has been extensively used in programme evaluation; in many cases, it is institutionalised. Even so, there appear to be occasional problems of response rate and statistical significance. There may also be sample design problems, especially in relation to the evaluation of indirect effects and networking. Programme participants are often very diverse and, in some cases, not fully known to programme sponsors. Perhaps more importantly, surveys need to be designed in relation to articulated hypotheses, and for indirect effects these remain difficult to formulate (BETA, 1988 and 1993).

In addition, there may be incentives to prove that the programme has met its goals. Most institutionalised surveys are primarily concerned with programme management. There is also the more general issue of how to formulate survey questions (or conduct interviews) that can identify longer-term impacts, especially on the diffusion of technologies and the development of networks. While it may not seem ideal, surveying can produce important results. Some of the surveys include non-participants as a control group.

With the evaluation of the Australian fiscal programme performed by the Bureau of Industry Economics (1989), the initial impact was measured through three surveys: of firms registered for the concession, of research institutions, and of R&D-performing manufacturers not registered. The evaluation recognises that the impact of the scheme on the Australian economy through the commercialisation of innovations cannot be measured until some time has elapsed.

One EC evaluation (Linne, 1991) has considered the impacts of BRITE/EURAM programmes on industrial networking, distinguishing between large and small numbers of programme participants. Two hundred and twenty-four projects were selected, based on 445 EC contracts, and a very high response rate (85 per cent) was achieved in detailed surveying. The focus was on the effectiveness (adequacy) of research programme features, the efficiency of international co-operation, and the nature of interfirm co-operation. However, the focus of analysis was primarily on programme management rather than impacts.

The use of patent data

Much has been (and continues to be) published on the use of patent data as an indicator for technology innovation and diffusion (EC, 1991; OECD, 1993; and Schankerman, 1991). However, its use in evaluating impacts of government technology programmes poses special problems. On the one hand, it could serve as an early and quantifiable proxy indicator of programme outputs,[16] which might also address the technology diffusion and national competitiveness issues. On the other hand, to the extent that patent data is usable as a technology indicator, it focuses on successful appropriation of R&D results. Government programmes have different concerns: how far should these results be appropriated rather than retained as public goods? Are formal programmes the best way to promote appropriation?

So far there has been little attempt to explore the use of patent data in the evaluation of government programmes [excepting EC programmes (see EC, 1991 and Grupp, Schmoch and Kuntze, 1991), but even these efforts do not really address the problems of differing objectives mentioned above]. It may therefore be inappropriate here to discuss the use of patent data as a measure of technology innovation, technology diffusion or national competitiveness, apart from making a couple of observations.

First, the use of patenting to appropriate technology innovation varies between technologies and industrial sectors – and probably, between countries as well (Levin et al., 1987). Secondly, the Yale I surveys suggest that in the United States, patenting has only modest importance as a firm appropriation strategy, and is considerably behind other strategies (secrecy, lead time, moving quickly along the learning curve, sales or service efforts). Patenting is more important for products than processes. This is probably also true for other countries.

Of the seven studies reviewed in the EC report, only two – Germany (Meyer-Krahmer, 1984) and Japan (Tanaka, 1989) – found patenting to be a useful indicator. The central problem was that very few patents could be linked with specific programme participants, which hinders statistical analysis. More generally, there was no easy way of addressing causality/additionality from government intervention.

Another technical problem concerns the time required for programme participants to apply for patents and their subsequent approval. The EC report suggests that "patentable results... are expected to turn out a year or two after the (work) has started", but that there may be a time-lag of "two to four years before (foreign trade) effects" are identifiable.

The BETA (1993) evaluation of EC BRITE/EURAM programmes used survey participants' estimates of the amount that they had spent to register and maintain patents as a proxy for the minimum value of their (indirect) benefits.

Problems aside, patent applications remain a relatively early and objective indicator for some programme results. The EC report proposes that they should be incorporated into the institutionalisation of government programme evaluation.

Chapter 4

Impacts – overview of empirical results

Introduction

The methodological problems of macro-economic quantitative assessment of national technology programmes are formidable. The econometric research reviewed in Chapter 3 indicates that national economic returns to R&D are higher than private returns to R&D or returns to private investment in general. While there may be clear evidence of market failure, econometric studies cannot conclusively show that government R&D finance mitigates this failure. It *probably* does; on balance, it appears that the results of government intervention are economically positive. The lack of either uniform results or firm conclusions stems from the difficulty of identifying and handling government R&D inputs – especially defence and government procurement – and, on the output side, from the difficulty of tracing effects, particularly those of externalities and spillovers.

Much of the economical analysis of government R&D programmes is challenged by the fact that industrial innovation occurs in oligopolistic markets with actors of unequal size. Capron and Debande (1993) explore the extent to which games theoretical approaches can contribute to the analysis. They review several existing studies: however, for most of these government is not a primary actor. So, the conclusions summarised in Table 15 are sceptical, but they point the need to greater evaluation which reflects the role of governments in oligopolistic markets.

Moreover, the available analysis – both cross-sectional and time series – relates to data that are usually 10 to 15 years old. Government support policies and the economic conjuncture have changed. Indeed, in view of the absence of conclusive *quantitative* results with regard to *overall* government technology efforts, what would seem to be needed is more *qualitative* and detailed investigation of *specific* programmes.

Earlier chapters have shown how assessment of impacts is conditioned by the "programme process":

- Apart from a handful of exceptions in a few (large) countries, identifiable programmes represent only a small part of overall government efforts to promote R&D, and R&D is only part of the innovation process.
- Identifiable programmes have complex and conflicting objectives, which can only partially be interpreted in terms of the technology objectives outlined in Chapter 2.

Table 15. **Pros and cons of alternative policies**

Advantages	Disadvantages
1. Direct or indirect subsidies to restore incentives	
– Effective in markets where technological spillovers are high	– Insufficient dissemination of uncorrected R&D results – Moral hazard, *i.e.* the government has no information about the cost structure of the firm – Additional taxes to be levied
2. Strengthening incentives to engage in *ex post* co-operation	
– Incentive to conduct R&D because they allow a firm to appropriate the benefits of innovation more fully – Better diffusion due to improved information control exerted by the innovator	– Limit the possible spillover and thus the efficient sharing of R&D – Reduction in R&D investment incentives for non first-generation innovators – Risk of cartel by using licensing contracts in a downstream product market
3. Encouraging greater *ex ante* co-operation	
– Greater amount of R&D investment: internalises the externalities created by technological spillovers, while continuing efficient information-sharing – Greater efficiency of R&D investment: more R&D projects are started due to cost-sharing; the effective amount of R&D is higher; intangible assets are shared, financial problems resolved and there is compensation for the lack of insurance against the failure of an R&D investment due to moral hazard; eliminates wasteful duplication	– Intense rivalry between the different firms at the competitive stage

Source: Capron and Debande, 1993, Table 2.

- Formal evaluation of programmes is largely driven by considerations of management and public accountability, neither of which are the main subject of this paper.

Consequently, it is important to recognise the biases and unreliability that come from the available analysis:

- Because of costs and institutional constraints, evaluation may be biased towards large or politically "visible" programmes, or programmes for which evaluation is relatively straightforward.
- Evaluation requires the active and willing response of participants. The more detailed and probing the evaluation, the less likely it is that participants will co-

operate. Alternatively, participants may have an incentive to give self-serving positive responses.

- Evaluation of commercial outcomes (and therefore of competitiveness issues) may raise problems of data confidentiality.
- It is difficult to predict long-term outcomes, which may inhibit participant response, and bias results towards predictable outcomes.

The "independence" of programme evaluations thus remains an intractable problem. There is a trade-off between generating programme data (through the institutionalisation of the process) and the reliability of the data generated. "Arm's-length" evaluation is more independent and can address the wider technology issues, but is relatively expensive (again, leading to biases in what is evaluated) and creates major data problems, such as non-co-operation by programme participants and a greater reliance on "proxy" indicators.

The central causality problem, linked to the justification issues outlined in Chapter 1, is the most daunting. Very few evaluations have adequately answered the core questions: what would have happened without the programme? How far were programme outcomes the result of the programme?

The available evaluation findings for typical programmes are presented below under five headings: raising overall R&D efforts, economic evaluation – market failure, promotion of innovation, national innovation systems and diffusion, and international issues.

Raising overall R&D efforts

Most OECD Member countries provide indirect incentives with the objective of raising overall levels of national R&D. There have been several studies of the effectiveness of fiscal programmes in inducing additional R&D expenditures (Bureau of Industry Economics, 1989; Hall, 1992; OECD, 1990a). Subsidies to R&D personnel in SMEs are discussed below. Bearing in mind that the following paragraphs touch on difficulties in evaluation that also hold for other government R&D programmes, the issues are:

  i) How much additional R&D is induced in relation to lost government revenue?
  ii) What are the net national economic benefits of the additional R&D?

With regard to i), wider studies of the determinants of enterprise R&D suggest that "costs" are indeed an important factor in decisions to initiate R&D programmes, and therefore in overall R&D expenditures. However, this factor appears to be clearly interconnected to expectations about results which are a far more important criterion – for example, about the permanence of the fiscal incentive. Enterprise decisions about additional R&D investment are generally based on a longer-term time horizon for new R&D programmes, while governments have sometimes been unwilling to commit themselves to fiscal experiments for more than two or three years.

The net after-tax effects of fiscal concessions with regard to reducing R&D costs are typically much less than the nominal effects. The present and expected future tax position of potential participants is important [see *e.g.* Bureau of Industry Economics (1989) for Australia, and Swenson (1992) for the United States]. This is particularly important for SMEs but may also apply in a cyclical context, or to firms facing structural shifts.

Analysis is limited in that it relies primarily on surveying programme participants and (to some extent) non-participants. There seem to be difficult definition problems: some studies have found that, at least in the short run, fiscal programmes induce considerable "creative accounting" and reclassification.[17] Other findings suggest that these problems are generally of a short-term nature and of limited extent. The Bureau of Industry Economics (1989) Australian evaluation pointed to the difficulty of analysing additionality in a context of rising aggregate enterprise R&D.[18] Econometric analysis is also limited by the need to eliminate trend and structural effects.

Most studies conclude that the ratio of induced R&D to foregone government revenue may be around 0.3-0.4 (Bureau of Industry Economics, 1989; Cordes, 1989). An official survey of international programmes performed by the UK Treasury concluded that "special fiscal incentives increase R&D by an amount that is roughly one-half of the revenue foregone by the government: the remainder goes to swell companies' cash flow and post-tax profits" (Stoneman, 1991). For Australia, the overall (short-term) results seem to have been less satisfactory: a ratio of 0.25:1.[19] However, the latter results should not be interpreted too negatively.[20]

Recent US analysis, based on most recent methodology and longer data time series, suggests much more positive results. According to Hall (1992), "the average price elasticity for R&D spending... is in the neighbourhood of unity in the short term". Implicitly, it is considerably higher for the longer term. The US experience is very special. Fiscal incentives have been restricted to additional R&D expenditures; they have not been considered as permanent (and there may have been enterprise considerations about offshore treatment of domestic R&D expenditures). Those facts may or may not account for the higher elasticities of enterprise R&D response in the United States. In any case elasticities close to unity would make fiscal incentives a relatively cost-efficient method of raising overall national R&D expenditures.

Regarding the impacts of additionality [*ii)* above], there are wider evaluation problems. One is to establish how far the additional R&D can be assimilated to other enterprise R&D, a variable involving the motivations and expectations of enterprises, and the types of R&D additionally promoted. Very little evidence has emerged from available evaluations. It is implicitly assumed that the additional R&D is assimilated to other enterprise R&D.

If this is so, the resulting national economic impacts can be assimilated to those of enterprise R&D. There is considerable evidence that they are much higher than private returns to investment in general. However, to the extent that the issue is the return to government investment (loss of government revenues), the calculation needs to take account of the limited additionality (0.3-0.4). If administration and deadweight costs are included, national economic returns to government investment in R&D through fiscal programmes would need to be at least three, and perhaps up to six, times higher than market returns to justify government intervention.

More generally, there is interest in assessing how much indirect (especially fiscal) incentives can promote an "innovation culture" and better diffusion and networking. The fiscal incentive would be transmitted from those that can benefit directly to those who cannot. Stability of enterprise expectations and (therefore) programmes are important conditions here. There is almost no evidence on this in the available evaluation reports. The Bureau of Industry Economics (1989) survey results did indicate that some additional collaborative R&D resulted from the concession scheme. Meyer-Krahmer (1987) found very limited effects from R&D personnel subsidies to SMEs in Germany.

Given the diffuse nature of these indirect measures to promote aggregate R&D, there is little evidence regarding their effects on national competitiveness. In the Bureau of Industry Economics (1989) analysis, the few foreign-owned respondents reported that the concession had had little effect on the transfer of R&D operations to Australia.

Economic evaluation – market failure

The review of econometric analysis above confirms the presence of market failure, but does not confirm that government intervention to finance R&D has corrected it. It suggests that government programmes have generally been additional to private R&D, but not that they have generated much extra private R&D. This explains the interest in analysing particular programmes. As noted above (Chapter 2 and Table 6), as much as two-thirds of Canadian federal R&D in 1986-87 could be judged to be directed towards correcting market failure, primarily inappropriability.

In formal cost/benefit analysis, the economic costs (especially deadweight costs) of national programmes are considerable, and much higher for direct programmes than for indirect (fiscal) programmes. For direct programmes (loans and grants), they could be twice the nominal costs.

Assessing benefits is more difficult. The question of risk is very important here. Provided that the benefits of a successful programme are substantial a few successes could justify many failures.

In his analysis of six EC BRITE near-market programmes, Toulemonde (1990) found very large potential gains. However, the spread in gains between programmes was considerable. Expectations of failure were also considerable, although in the socio-economic (market) rather than the technical domain. The results are summarised in Table 11.[21]

The technology appropriation issues are tough ones. First, there are uncertainties about how firms in different sectors or other participants in national programmes appropriate and use the results of their R&D activities (Levin et al., 1987). Secondly, why should appropriation be a measure of programme success and who should appropriate the outputs? More important than the justification for government intervention is the creation and dissemination of knowledge in the public domain.

A few national programme evaluations have used patents as a proxy for programme outputs and success. In its four CSIRO evaluations, the Bureau of Industry Economics

(1992) judged that although all the programmes were socially profitable, none would have had a positive cost/benefit ratio if benefits had been valued at prospective returns to the government from the sale of intellectual property rights.

The major French study of the impacts in France of EC programmes (Laredo and Callon, 1990) reached negative conclusions regarding classical market failure justifications. Recipients of EC grants "only rarely" reoriented their existing research themes and "almost never" took up risky projects. The major positive impacts related to the strengthening of TENs and reorientation of the configurations and focus of existing research.

Folster's (1988) analysis points to the importance of information on private and social profits in evaluating government programmes. Table 16, based on a simulation analysis of 30 projects, suggests important social gains for all types of government intervention, but much greater gains for conditional loans and incentive subsidies than for normal grants. The benefits are assessed in relation to market failure criteria; the analysis suggests that there are substantial increases in "social value" due to government R&D subsidies, but that these are very much dependent on the quality of government information about *ex ante* and *ex post* private and social profitability. The table suggests that the major advantage of conditional loans and incentive subsidies over normal grants is their ability to disqualify from government support R&D that firms would in any case have conducted without the support (ensuring additionality).[22]

Folster (1988), however, argues strongly that "conditional loans" (where repayment is conditional on programme results) are clearly preferable to fixed grants (decided in advance of launching specific R&D projects). One general reason is that *ex post* information on completed R&D programmes – which can influence the extent of repayment – will normally be better than *ex ante* information, on which grant decisions are based. It is further argued that conditional loans are a more cost-efficient instrument for meeting the risk justification for government intervention.

He proposes a further policy step, "incentive subsidies", where payments would depend on programme outcomes – the level of private and social profits and the relation-

Table 16. **Percentage increase in social value over non-subsidised activities**

	Perfect information	Small government error	Large government error	Systematic government error
1. Incentive subsidy	26	23	16	9
2. Normal subsidy	19	12	–6	2
3. Conditional loan	22	17	5	5
4. Hypothetical perfectly incentive compatible subsidy	28	25	19	12

Source: Folster, 1988.

ship between them. Private profits would be deducted from the subsidy, thereby discouraging firms from applying for grants for R&D that would be undertaken in any case. Performing firms would receive some percentage of social profits, which would encourage them to undertake socially useful R&D. Risk would be insured, in the sense that unsuccessful R&D would be reimbursed while financially profitable R&D would not.

This argument about the welfare efficiency of traditional grants, conditional loans and incentive subsidies should not imply government targeting or choice of R&D programmes. What is required is *ex post* assessment of private and social profitability, which together determine the subsidy amount. It also requires *ex ante* assessment of how much subsidy is likely to be required, so that rates can be determined.

Incentive subsidy schemes do not appear to have been used thus far. Even if targeting and detailed government views on the merits of particular R&D investments are not required, the system would be relatively data-demanding, implying something approaching an *ex post* social cost/benefit analysis. Folster argues, however, that for any given level of data and evaluation possibilities, a conditional grant system – and, still more, an incentive system – must be more efficient than normal grants. Table 16 gives some expected results from a simulation exercise.

In analysis of US Department of Energy (DOE) programmes, the choice of strategy employed seemed to be important to success in commercialisation, and depended strongly on the characteristics of the government programme in terms of technology, and market and policy criteria (Table 17, and Brown *et al.*, 1991). On the basis of the programmes analysed, which were limited in number and range, the most important commercialisation strategy was clearly that of the national laboratory "contracting R&D to industrial partners", followed by "generating end-user demand" and "influencing key decision-makers".

To some extent, the analysis is oriented towards technological spin-offs, and certainly the R&D involved was near-market. In every case there was market failure, which was corrected by government intervention. Market failure was in several instances due to non-appropriability – imitation would be too easy – and was partly resolved by public/contractor appropriation, but partly also through keeping the technology in the public domain.

Market failure was clearly corrected by public intervention in five out of the nine cases, since products/processes had achieved viable/successful market acceptability at the time of evaluation. In the remaining four, the intended commercial results had not yet been satisfactorily achieved. The authors suggest that this may have been due to inappropriate commercialisation strategies.

Promotion of innovation

National technology programmes vary considerably in the extent to which they target specific technologies or industries. The TEP arguments in Chapter 1 suggest that governments may legitimately wish to promote specific technology trajectories and seek

Table 17. Linkages between evaluation criteria and technology transfer strategies [1]

	Contracting R&D to industrial partners	Working with industrial consortia	Licensing to industry	Influencing key decision-makers	Working with broker organisations	Generating end-user demand
Technological criteria:						
Nature of technology						
Process	H	S	S	H	S	S
Product			S	S		H
Nature of R&D						
Exploratory	S	H	S	S	H	H
Applied	H	S		H	S	S
Complexity						
Simple	H		S			
Complex	H	S	H		S	H
Nature of information						
Proprietary	H		S	H	S	
Non-proprietary	S			H		
Technological uncertainty						
Low	S	H		S	S	H
High	H		S	S		H
Market criteria:						
Breadth of applications						
Unified	H		S			H
Diverse	H		S			S
Nature of industry						
Competitive						S
Concentrated	H	H		H		H
Policy criteria:						
Government support						
Limited	H	S	S	H	S	S
Abundant	S	S		S	S	H
Desired time-line						
Normal	H			H	S	S
Accelerated	S				S	H

1. H = highly appropriate; S = sometimes appropriate.
Source: Brown et al., 1991, p. 138.

"winners". In the more general sense of targeting, they have frequently done so. One can distinguish:

  i) Large programmes targeted to specific technology objectives. However, most of these dominant programmes have not had primarily industrial objectives – or at best, have had implicit dual-use objectives.
  ii) Programmes targeted more generally at technologies judged to be "generic", "emerging", "critical", "enabling" or "strategic".

The very notion of targeting is imprecise, as is illustrated by the EUREKA programme. The general objectives of EUREKA are clearly the development of generic technologies and European competitiveness, but the choice and development of specific programmes are very much left to programme participants.

There are important questions about how successful the few large programmes have been and about how far they have "crowded-out" other programmes/technology alternatives. Because they were conceived and developed in specific historical and economic contexts – at the time, they were seen as strategic technology options – it is unclear how far lessons can be drawn for future programmes in relation to what are now perceived as "critical" technologies.

Targeted large programmes

Ergas (1993) argues that a very small number of large targeted programmes have dominated the government R&D efforts of some large countries (*e.g.* France, Germany, and the United Kingdom). However, most of these dominant programmes have not had primarily industrial objectives, or have had implicit dual-use objectives. He points to two disappointing UK efforts, Concorde and the nuclear AGR alternative: "the net economic loss to the UK... measured in today's currency, exceeds $20 billion – an amount equal to nearly two years of all British R&D expenditure in the late 1980s". For Germany, he claims that "throughout the first half of the 1980s, two projects – the SNR 300 Fast Breeder Reactor... and the high temperature reactor...absorbed fully 30 per cent of direct R&D funding provided by the BMFT (Federal Ministry for Research and Technology)". Moreover, in spite of a BFMT concern to promote SMEs, the share of the very largest firms in BMFT funding remained very large.

Apart from purely military objectives, these very large programmes primarily concerned aircraft development (including civilian SST), space technology and nuclear technology (see *e.g.* Ergas, 1993 and Alic *et al.,* 1992, Chapter 7). More recently, some aspects of information technology have generated programmes of this size (*e.g.* OECD, 1989*b* and Alvey, 1991). A few other civilian technologies (notably high-speed rail transport) were also important.

In a few large countries (France, the United States, the United Kingdom and perhaps Germany, Japan and Sweden) these technologies were seen as "strategic", in the broad sense of military survival or national energy independence. For Europe, the strategic notion concerned the capability to develop a viable technology that could withstand US and (subsequently) Japanese competition. However, the strategic concerns were mainly military (or, for nuclear technology, about national economic self-sufficiency). There is considerable literature (Alic *et al.,* 1992; Branscomb, 1992; NAS, NAE and IOM, 1992) on how far these concerns intertwined with less strategic national economic concerns.

Much can be learned from the mega-programmes of the 1960-80 period, because they institutionalised procedures for the choice and development of programmes. The negative (non-strategic) balance sheet certainly provides lessons about targeting technology trajectories. The SST programmes in the United States (Cohen and Noll, 1991), and the United Kingdom/France (Henderson, 1977) were in retrospect a massive misuse of national technological efforts that inhibited the development of other more promising projects (especially wide-body, low-cost aircraft – for a discussion of the misconceived competition at Boeing between the 747 and the SST, see Irving, 1993), and probably (at least in Europe) diverted funds from other technology. However, the failure was primarily commercial, not technological: the US SST failed to meet its technological objectives, and by the time the less technologically-demanding European SST was ready, there was no market.

In nuclear energy, of the (perhaps) six promising technologies developed in the 1960s and 1970s, only one (the Westinghouse PWR) has had commercial success, largely because the French government abandoned its own national technology programme in favour of it (Ergas, 1993). Again, as suggested in the TEP trajectory analysis, commercial success was not due to any inherent technological superiority of the PWR technology. Exogenous events – falling energy prices, global recession and perceived fears of nuclear technology – largely destroyed the market in the late 1970s and 1980s, except in France.

This does not mean that other national nuclear programmes were a total waste of public R&D resources: national capabilities have been developed which are now yielding spin-offs, and there could be future markets for other nuclear technologies. However, it is doubtful whether in retrospect present spin-offs or ultimate developments could have justified the original government programmes in either economic or political terms. It is doubtful whether governments would have initiated the budgets or the resulting R&D institutions if they had correctly anticipated the outcomes.

Major government efforts were also devoted to developing high-speed rail transport in France (the TGV), Japan, the United Kingdom, Italy and Germany. Here, there are basic system choices – completely new dedicated tracks (the TGV), adaptation to existing tracks (Germany, Italy, the United Kingdom), or completely new technology (MAGLEV, also involving dedicated tracks) – which are only partly about basic technology choices. The commercial success of the French TGV reflects government commitment beyond the initial technology development phase (essentially government procurement, infrastructure development and, perhaps, cross-subsidisation in pricing policy).

It should be noted that such programmes have typically involved the government or parastatal institutions as initial purchasers, with some government guarantee that the technology would be carried through to commercial success. This situation is now changing. More importantly, the new critical technologies have different market characteristics. Ergas (1993) has argued, for example, that the French government has had much less success with national technology programmes (*e.g.* information technology), whose outputs are market-driven.

There has also been "locking-in" of participants around entrenched large programmes. As political priorities shift or R&D programmes develop, participants shift the objectives but retain the programme structures and funding. Ergas argues that this is an issue in France, where there is a small technological elite involved in the programmes and complicity between funders and performers. It has similarly been argued for the United Kingdom (Gummett, 1992) that aircraft R&D programmes became part of wider industrial policies to restructure the aerospace industry in the 1960s and 1970s. The US Brookings study (Cohen and Noll, 1991) is very much concerned with how the "pork-barrel" political process came to dominate decisions about the future life of six large programmes dependent on Congressional approval for annual funding.

The corollary of locking-in is the crowding-out of other programmes. On this, little evidence is available. Ergas (1987) argues that given the sheer size of US technological efforts, the risk of crowding-out by individual programmes is much less than in (even) large European countries. He also argues that the institutionalisation of government support to industry in Japan has so far led to relative flexibility in adjusting to emerging technology priorities. For Europe, by contrast, in countries that are both "mission-oriented" (France, the United Kingdom) and "diffusion-oriented" (Germany), government technology programmes have become increasingly ill-adapted to changing technology priorities, especially in the realm of new generic technologies.

The problems of exogenous events are clearly evident, and are documented in the six US cases reviewed in Cohen and Noll (1991). International energy price developments and associated energy policy shifts had a devastating effect on programmes to develop synthetic fuels and efficient photovoltaic solar devices. The problem was not that the research was unsuccessful, but that its annual funding was influenced by energy and industrial policy considerations. In the case of the Applications Technology Satellite Programme the research was also largely successful, but the programme was aborted mainly because industry came to judge that it could appropriate the benefits of continuing research, although programme sponsors judged that there was still public interest/externalities in continuing a publicly-financed programme.

The French authorities have recently released a highly critical report on the space programmes of the *Centre national d'études spatiales* (CNES), review by the *Comité national d'évaluation de la recherche* (CNER, 1992). The report well illustrates the issues that arise with large targeted national programmes:

i) The Ariane 4 rocket programme is a technological success, but its initial commercial success was partly the result of the failure of the US Challenger programme (in 1986) and the breakup of the USSR: there is now the prospect of overcapacity in the global satellite launching market, with renewed competition from the United States, Russia and China, aggravated in the important telecommunications market by developments in fibreoptics technology.

ii) The envisaged objectives and risks for the new programmes were too great for an individual national effort, and became inextricably linked to those of the wider programmes of the European Space Agency (ESA), in which France's central budget share is only 18 per cent. In the face of reluctance from other

ESA members and France's determination and technological lead in (at least) launch technology, *ad hoc* arrangements were made for Ariane 5 (the launch rocket); Columbus (a space station); a European module for an international space laboratory (Freedom) which would link European, US, Japanese and Russian efforts; and Hermes, which would carry astronauts to the space laboratory. These ad hoc arrangements left France in charge of the Ariane 5 and Hermes programmes, but involved a French budget participation of almost 50 per cent and problematic compensatory arrangements.

iii) The technological problems and risks for the ongoing programmes are daunting. The performance specifications for Ariane 5 have been raised (they were already several orders of magnitude greater than Ariane 4), while the useful projected carrying capabilities of Hermes have been reduced to the point where CNER doubts whether there will be a market for a European manned space initiative.

iv) The Ariane programme has led the CNES into financing major operational infrastructure activities in French Guyana, and Ariane 5 envisages further activities on a massive scale (including the creation of facilities for supplying new booster engines not required by Ariane 4). These infrastructure investments seem to come from the national budget for civilian R&D, although the CNER report is not clear on that point.

v) The CNES budget seems to represent around one-third of the total French budget for civilian R&D. The CNER report does not discuss the possible crowding-out effects on non-space R&D, but is concerned that even the client space S&T community was not adequately consulted about the strategic options and has misgivings about the orientations adopted (*e.g.* the importance/feasibility of manned micro-gravity experiments).

vi) The CNER found evidence of creative accounting in which R&D staff costs were funded from equipment budgets. More generally, in contrast to the US pork-barrel process (Cohen and Noll, 1991), there seems to have been very little public parliamentary discussion of objectives or budgets, with the political lobbies that this would entail: the CNER complaint is, rather, that the development of programmes and options was internalised within CNES, with less than satisfactory peer review of scientific options and inadequate administrative review of budgets or strategic options.

vii) The CNER report is sceptical about externalities and diffusion effects. It considered the extent to which the special conditions and requirements of space research promoted materials, systems or software which could not otherwise have been developed, which found applications, or which were promoted, outside the space sector. It found that "in the light of the many studies consulted and having asked its own experts to analyse the importance of technology fallouts in their own domain, no significant new case was detected, at least outside the aerospatial world itself. Spatial solutions are in general much too costly to be applied elsewhere, they are also not adapted to series production, etc. Space, at least at the level of the current European programme, has no longer a monopoly of complex and costly projects, forcing technology beyond its existing limits..." It argued (in parallel with recent US discussions about dual-use technologies – see NAS, NAE and IOM, 1992; and Alic *et al.,* 1992) that the focus was now on "spin-ons" rather than on spin-offs.

viii) It also found very little mobility of staff between the CNES and other institutions; this was seen as a staffing problem for CNES, but it could also be seen as a technology diffusion problem.

ix) The *juste retour*: the CNER report was troubled that as a result of the complicated arrangements mentioned in *ii)* above, non-French institutions/firms (especially UK firms) are being financed from French contributions to the ESA.

Generic technologies

In the area of generic technologies, there is clear market failure justification for government support in the sense that *i)* the beneficial impacts are downstream from the innovators; *ii)* the government is justified in picking winners; and *iii)* more generally, there are externalities to the programme. Environment-related programmes represent a special case of technology promoted to yield a non-appropriable public good (Heaton *et al.,* 1992; Branscomb, 1993). Information technology programmes are discussed in OECD, 1989*b*.

Most OECD Member countries have programmes supporting these technologies, which come with a variety of labels and objectives. Most concern biotechnology, electronics or new materials. Because their impacts are likely to be long-term and pervasive, they have proved difficult to evaluate.

The UK Alvey Programme for Information Technology can be seen as an attempt to start afresh with new objectives and new structures (in evaluation, among other domains). It was set up as a five-year programme of pre-competitive research to be performed as collaborative projects between firms and public sector research, sponsored by several ministries. Total government funding was £200 million, with industry contributing a further £150 million. The evaluation report (Alvey, 1991) considers the technical, structural and strategic achievements of the programme. It largely attained its technical objectives. The impact on the structure of the UK IT sector was significant: the R&D base was broadened and a platform for exploitation was established. The population of IT researchers was increased, and the quality and extent of links between different members of the IT community improved over the course of the programme, particularly between academia and industry. (The benefits of the links accrued more to industry than to academics.) The majority of participants built upon Alvey R&D in the context of follow-up research projects.

Impacts on the industrial competitiveness of the UK IT sector were less clear-cut. The programme supported pre-competitive research, and it was not intended that the projects should lead directly to production. However, it was expected that some results would be used to improve production processes and enhance product development. It was found that the extent and scale of the barriers to exploitation as a result of the strategic shifts of industrial partners were higher than could have been anticipated at the outset. Other barriers to exploitation were poor management of the interface between R&D and production, and a shortage of capital necessary to move into production. The longer-term impact of Alvey on the competitiveness and commercial performance of the UK IT sector may be hampered by these factors.

The evaluation concluded that collaborative pre-competitive R&D programmes are insufficient on their own, as the different phases of the innovation process which could be supported by government technology policies were not present. The impact of future programmes would be enhanced by complementary support measures, including the involvement of users, encouragement of better technology strategy in firms, and the facilitation of capital for commercial exploitation.

Small countries

Small countries face particular problems with targeted programmes – especially for generic technologies – and with the evaluation of their impacts. There are linked concerns:

    i) critical mass in the R&D and dispersion of scarce resources;
    ii) the targeting of present or future industrial competitive advantages;
    iii) the scope, risks and legitimacy of free-riding;
    iv) "nationality", essentially the participation of non-national firms in government-financed R&D;
    v) the need for international participation in evaluation.

Several evaluations yield interesting if partial conclusions on such small-country programmes. Ireland has several recent Programmes for Advanced Technology (PATs). In the Quo-Tec evaluation of the BioResearch Ireland (BRI) programme, which seeks to promote university/industry links in biotechnology, the overall conclusion was very positive. The projects have in general evolved in clear response to prospective specific industry needs, although industry has participated financially somewhat less than expected. The prospective economic returns are very positive, especially in terms of skilled employment. There is clear additionality. Nationality was not seen as a problem: Ireland has good prospects for inward investment. The reservations are about the possible dispersion of R&D activity in BRI's university-based "centres", and about the future institutional structure of the programme and/or BRI. It should be added that much of the funding comes ultimately from EC programmes, and that (in this area) Ireland has no problems about the *juste retour*. The evaluation, conducted by a consulting group, involved international experts and, where possible, comparison with other programmes.

National innovation systems and diffusion

It is very difficult to assess the impacts of national technology programmes on innovation systems and technology diffusion through the available formal programme evaluations. Some programmes have had technology diffusion as a central objective, and a few have been evaluated from this standpoint. However, as argued in Chapter 4, the assessment problems are formidable. Most evaluation is limited to the principal programme participants (or, in some cases, potential non-participants), but not to other actors not formally involved. Some case materials which illustrate the evaluation problem but which generally show positive benefits to government programmes are presented below.

It was stated earlier that one justification for government intervention could be to mitigate market failure through excessive transaction costs, and that a legitimate government role could be to promote R&D collaboration (networking) rather than either greater public supply of R&D results (as a public good) or greater toleration of technological appropriation (IPR, which would involve the risk of greater oligopolisation or mono-polisation of product or process markets). It is important to note that such R&D collaboration will involve conflicts of interest among participants as well as a scope for collective benefits. The government's role then becomes partly that of promoting "positive" collaborative behaviour and discouraging non-collaborative free-riders.

The EC evaluation of BRITE/EURAM programmes reported by Linne was based on detailed surveying of industrial programme participants, and contains strategic recommendations for further programmes. These are primarily about overall programme management, but they suggest conclusions about impacts which are fairly negative (1991, pp. 12-13). Essentially, they recommend a "bottom-up" approach in selecting both firms and technologies to support, but also greater EC financial participation (60 per cent), better targeting (support for core projects), and a relative shift from large to smaller firms.

The Canadian IRAP programme (Chapter 2) was assessed in 1990 by the National Research Council, which manages the programme. The evaluation addresses the use of IRAP by private sector firms and analyses the types of project supported. The impact of the programme is approached from the perspective of client relevance, since IRAP is there to assist firms in raising their levels of technological competence and awareness. More than 86 per cent of clients surveyed identified positive changes in their technical capability over the past four years, and 90 per cent credited IRAP with a major role in that improvement. Firms appeared to value both the financial assistance and the technical advice. More than 60 per cent of those surveyed (500 firms) stated that the advice was at least as important as the funding. Sixty per cent of firms reported increased sales or cost reductions, with an average increase of C$ 200 000 for the first year after project completion, and 15 per cent reported cost savings (averaging C$ 30 000 for the first year). There was a measurable difference in firm success and growth between non-IRAP and IRAP-assisted firms, although it was not large and would have to be confirmed by a larger sample. Additionality of IRAP assistance was investigated by asking firms what the impact of not receiving IRAP assistance would have been, whether they could have gone ahead without IRAP, and whether there were alternatives to IRAP. More than 65 per cent of firms surveyed rated IRAP assistance as essential or important to the successful completion of their project (selection criteria encourage high additionality). The programme appeared to have an impact on R&D staff employment, as firms in all elements of IRAP reported an increase in their R&D staff since first contact with the programme. Forty per cent of students under IRAP assistance were hired by the firm once the project was completed.

An independent evaluation of the German Production Technology Programme performed during real time and *ex post* using a mix of methods (before/after comparisons, control group studies, case studies) looked at its achievements and impacts, including that of CAD/CAM on the productivity of manufacturing industry. Postal questionnaires and interviews were conducted with supported and non-supported firms. The evaluation found that the proportion of CAD users had approximately trebled over the programme (13 to 36 per cent), and the proportion of CAM users doubled (25 to 50 per cent). Eleven per cent of the firms said that they would not have tackled the project without the funding and 83 per cent said that the funding had brought their project forward in time, made it more comprehensive or enabled it to be completed sooner. The extent to which firms overvalue the positive aspects of funding is open to debate; case study analysis allowed deeper investigation. A free-rider effect was noted, because it was apparent that the programme triggered an interest from non-supported firms in CAD/CAM; the firms invested even without state support. An indirect impact of the scheme was artificial stimulation of the market, which was stagnant again at the end of the promotion.

Diffusion of public R&D

Many OECD countries have policy initiatives directed at better use of public research by firms, with the aims of increasing the commercial returns to government-funded R&D and enhancing national competitiveness and technology diffusion. Evaluation problems concern spin-offs from government laboratories and, more generally, dual-use of technologies principally developed with government finance for non-commercial objectives. The problems are monumental, and there have been very few specific attempts at assessment.

Much interest centres on the role of national research laboratories. Their significance in performing government-financed research is clear. They are under increasing financial and policy pressure to find commercial outputs and justifications for their activities. However, their role in relation to promoting industrial technology is generally fairly marginal to their principal activities.

For the United States, it has been argued (NAS, NAE and IOM, 1992) that most national laboratories are not appropriate institutions to promote technology commercialisation. There are some 700, with an overall budget in FY 1991 of almost US$21 billion, but most are very small and mission-oriented to very "upstream" research. The few promising ones are owned – but not managed – by the Defense and Energy Departments. Their record in transferring technology is "strikingly meagre" (op. cit., Table 2.2, based on GAO, 1991), in terms of patents, licences and royalties, and mainly concerns Defense and Energy Department laboratories.

In 1986, the United States established provisions for Co-operative Research and Development Agreements (CRADAs) between government-operated laboratories and industry. A CRADA is an agreement under which a private organisation provides person-nel, equipment or financing for specified R&D activity that complements the laboratory's mission. Between 1986 and 1991 almost 800 CRADAs were initiated, involving around 120 000 researchers (NAS, NAE and IOM, 1992): "The number of contracts signed between laboratories and firms does not indicate the utility of these agreements to meet specific technology objectives. It does show some limited progress in linking a few federal agency laboratories to industry through CRADAs''. Branscomb (1993) is similarly sceptical on using the number of CRADAs as an indicator of efficiency.

US commentators are generally approving of the technology transfer activities financed by the National Institutes of Health (NIH) programmes, seeing them as an important source of the present strength of the US biotechnology industry. ''Many of these joint projects have moved research results out of federal laboratories and into the market-place. One important reason for this success has been the high degree of interaction between researchers in separate organisations in the biomedical field. The critical interface necessary for successful transfer and adoption of the technology involved is people-to-people contact'' (NAS, NAE and IOM, 1992).

The Department of Energy has the most extensive programme in technology transfer to the commercial sector. The agency's multidisciplinary, contractor-operated laboratories are widely considered to be among the most promising federal facilities for technology commercialisation. There are nine multi-programme laboratories. Argonne, Brookhaven, Lawrence Berkeley, Oak Ridge, and Pacific Northwest emphasise energy R&D; Lawrence Livermore, Los Alamos, Sandia and Idaho Engineering are weapons laboratories. There are also smaller laboratories noted for their work in energy research and applications, including the Solar Energy Research Institute (SERI), the department's main laboratory for basic and applied R&D in solar and renewable energies. SERI's R&D programmes include close interaction with the private sector. The multidisciplinary nature of some DOE laboratories involves them in research and development in fields – e.g. electronics and advanced materials – that increasingly rely on advances in cross-cutting technologies.

The NAS, NAE, and IOM report concludes that: ''Over the past decade, Congress and the executive branch have attempted to make civilian technology development an explicit mission of the federal laboratories. Yet, as measured by the number of patents or the amount of royalties resulting from laboratory transfer activities, this mission has not been fulfilled. In fact, few federal inventions are transferred out of these laboratories. A congressional committee investigating progress in meeting these goals found technology transfer efforts to be 'under-staffed, under-directed, and only marginally focused'. One indication of the lack of success in forging close relationships is the small output of technologies licensed to the private sector from federally-sponsored R&D performed at the laboratories. For FY 1989, 297 research-oriented federal laboratories surveyed by the General Accounting Office produced only US$6.3 million in royalties and 676 patents.''

The Canadian Government has taken several initiatives. Its Programme for Industry/Laboratory Project (PILP) provided private enterprises with access to technology developed through the efforts of the National Research Council of Canada and other federal laboratories. Part of industry's cost in acquiring technology or expertise was met by the government (the budget for which was C$ 17 million). Evaluation of PILP concentrated on the effectiveness of technology transfer. The firms consulted felt that they needed to be in control of the technology acquired through PILP in order to exploit it. They desired continuity of government financing in order to carry through exploitation, and wished to acquire the technology at an early stage in order to allow time to formulate a business plan, and to adapt the technology to their own configurations for commercialisation. The evaluation noted the need for a good match between companies and technologies and for a multidisciplinary approach.

A report has studied nine energy-related near-market government programmes financed by the US Department of Energy; the focus is on different institutional techniques for bringing innovations to commercial use (Brown *et al.,* 1991). The report analyses the links between different possible institutional techniques and types of innovation. The results are presented in Table 17.

As the schema shows, the analysis identifies six "technology transfer strategies":
– contracting R&D to industrial partners;
– working with industrial consortia;
– licensing to industry;
– influencing key decision-makers;
– working with broker organisations;
– generating end-user demand.

It further identifies 18 detailed criteria for classifying government R&D programmes, under three main headings: technological, market and policy. Using a simple weighting system for these detailed criteria, it seeks to determine the most appropriate (combination of) technology transfer strategies. The resulting proposed transfer guidelines were found to have corresponded to actual experience with the five (out of nine) programmes that had achieved commercial success.

The authors emphasise (p. 143) that the "paper has focused on innovations sponsored by a government programme that had technology transfer as a primary goal, where Federal laboratories played a strong role, and where technological advances... were generally incremental rather than revolutionary". They suggest that further research and additional case studies would be required to make the methodology more operational.

Stability of programmes and financing seems an important issue in relation to the expectations of programme participants, and therefore their motivation to participate (NAS, NAE and IOM, 1992). With specific programmes, there are important start-up costs for some participants. On the other hand, in programme management and public finance terms, it seems important that programmes have a finite life, and that there be "sunset" clauses (Bureau of Industry Economics, 1989).

A key related issue concerns the contractual career situation and outlook of the researchers involved in pre-commercial and (especially) near-market technology programmes. To the extent that these programmes are not the primary objective of the institutions involved, the researchers are concerned about retaining their career status within the national research system even when involved in collaborative research with industry on specific technology programmes. This is particularly a problem for national laboratories whose primary mandate is research in non-industrial or non-competitive fields (most obviously health and agriculture, but also to some extent defence, space and energy). There is also the problem about involving non-government researchers with in-house R&D in government laboratories.

The NAS, NAE and IOM study argues that because of the institutional constraints for national laboratories to work successfully with industry on pre-commercial R&D, and the political constraints on funding specific technology programmes, there is need for a Civilian Technology Corporation, which would be a "private, quasi-governmental institution intended to guide financial support for middle-ground, pre-commercial R&D in key technology areas of significance to the US technology base" (1992, p. 128).

Dual-use technology programmes

Clearly, most government R&D is not specifically directed to promoting industrial technology, but much of it (in defence, energy, health and agriculture) is related to commercial processes and products. A growing policy concern – and the objective of several specific programmes – is to maximise use of government R&D to enhance national competitiveness in industrial technologies. This is especially a problem for the United States, given the high share of R&D devoted to non-industrial objectives.

The Defense Advanced Research Projects Agency (DARPA) was established in the United States in 1958. Benefiting from a rapid appropriation increase in the 1980s, it currently manages a US$1.43 billion annual budget that supports research and development in high-risk advanced technology with potential applications in military systems. It is primarily concerned with "early stage" development of new technologies. DARPA's effectiveness in relation to civilian technology, and its future in a world of declining defence expenditures, have been extensively reviewed (see *e.g.* NAS, NAE and IOM, 1992; Alic *et al.*, 1992; and Branscomb, 1993). Legislation passed by Congress in 1993 has converted DARPA to ARPA, giving it wider technology promotion functions.

Evaluations suggest that DARPA-funded projects have developed many advances in military technology, in fields such as advanced materials (carbon-carbon composites and complex ceramics), R&D computers, data communications and computer networks. In addition to their significant impact on US military technology, these programmes have had substantial spillover effects in commercial sectors. Much of DARPA's success, which may not be attainable in strict civilian domains, comes from: *i)* autocratic and efficient management, protected by Department of Defense (DOD) secrecy; *ii)* DOD's role as an interactive client for research results; and *iii)* the flexibility of its operations, which are not conducted in-house but contracted out to industry, universities, and the branches of the armed services.

However, leading-edge military technology is currently challenged – less by lack of innovation in defence sectors than by the performance of dual-use and commercial innovators in the private sector. Moreover, DARPA has increasingly illustrated the problems of an uncomfortably close relationship with government: uncertain budgets, micro-management and staffing problems.

Branscomb (1993, p. 91) argues that the shift from defence to civilian preoccupations implies sizeable institutional problems: the Clinton Administration's strategy is to shift as much as US$8 billion annually from military to civilian investment. Most of this is not R&D in any narrow sense. However, the strategy raises questions about how existing civil technology institutions (and indeed ARPA) will cope with major budget shifts. It also raises international competition policy issues: while defence R&D and procurement cannot be challenged (they are technology for public goods), the situation changes if they are shifted into the civil sector.

Spin-offs from nuclear energy (including emerging institutional arrangements) have been extensively analysed by the NEA (1993). In this case, the spin-offs were prompted mainly by the need to find alternative uses for nuclear capabilities. The NEA report is not concerned with the formal evaluation of these programmes or their costs, but presents considerable detail on different types of and instruments for spin-offs, and their associated institutional shifts.

Small and medium-sized enterprises (SMEs)

Most OECD Member countries have national programmes that support technology development in small and medium-sized enterprises (SMEs) but, these have not been widely evaluated. In many of them, support for SMEs is a secondary target; where it is a primary target, objectives and instruments are heterogeneous. A common assumption is that because SMEs are small and financially weak, they cannot afford a minimum investment in R&D or to take technological risks – two of the classic justifications for government support. Transaction costs for technology acquisition, diffusion and networking are relatively high; SMEs thus cannot adequately benefit from R&D externalities without government support – a further classic justification.

On the other hand, because SMEs are small but numerous, governments have special problems in developing and administering (specially targeted) programmes. Moreover, because of their precarious (and sometimes "grey" fiscal/legal) situation, SMEs are frequently mistrustful of government programmes.

OECD's recent analysis of technology and competitiveness in relation to SMEs (OECD, 1993 and Table 18 below) came to generally pessimistic conclusions regarding the effectiveness of government programmes: "Systematic evaluation of the many government programmes supporting transfer of technology to SMEs and improving their competitiveness is very clearly lacking. A few surveys do, however, shed light. SMEs rely on various sources of information according to the needs of the moment and the way the situation is developing. In France, for example, surveys have shown that most SMEs... are aware of the main government aid programmes. Yet, they make little use of them either because they have other sources, they do not obtain information suited to their requirements or they are mistrustful of the State" p. 76).

An evaluation of the UK SMART programme was performed by the Department of Trade and Industry's Assessment Unit in 1991 in order to examine the rationale of the scheme, its cost-effectiveness (including achievement of objectives) and its administration. The evaluation was conducted by interviewing administrators, private financiers, and successful and non-successful applicants. The desired impacts were that firms develop and make commercial successes out of supported products, and go on to further projects with finance from the private sector. The evaluation followed up previous winners, and found that of the 20 participating in the pilot phase, four were successfully selling products and eight others have prospects for doing so. A large proportion (75 per cent) of the winners completed their project within the year, and almost all within 15 months. The

Table 18. Examples of support programmes for transferring technology resources to SMEs in various OECD countries, 1986-89

Country	Programme	Administering authority	Costs covered
1. Programmes dealing with dissemination of technology			
Germany	Aid for improving performance	Central government RW/BMWi	Investment in increased productivity
	Loans, finance houses for equity participation in SMEs	Central governmentt ERP	Co-operation, expansion, innovation, restructuring
Austria	Aid for structural improvement	Buerges Company	Investment in innovation and company start-up
Denmark	Credit for small and very small enterprises	Ministry of Finance	Start-up, modernisation costs
Spain	Aid to professional organisations providing services to SMEs	Ministry for Industry and Energy	R&D and advisory service costs
	Aid to SMEs in respect of quality and modernity of design	Ministry for Industry and Energy	50% of R&D, design/ quality and training costs
	Quality improvement	Ministry for Industry and Energy	Share of investment in quality management and improvement
United States	Small Business Innovation Research (SBIR)	SBA	R&D work for obtaining government contracts
	Support programme for energy-related inventions	Departments of Commerce and Energy	R&D costs for non-nuclear energy technology
France	Regional assistance for advanced manufacturing projects	Regions	20% of innovative production system costs for pilot schemes presenting regional interest
United Kingdom	Innovation-related investment	Department of Trade and Industry	Launching of products and of new or substantially-improved processes
Italy	Investment aid to SMEs in Southern Italy	Central government	Investment costs for new plant and modernisation
	Aid for purchase and leasing of high-tech equipment	Central government	High-tech machine tool purchase and leasing costs

Table 18. Examples of support programmes for transferring technology resources to SMEs in various OECD countries, 1986-89 *(cont'd)*

Country	Programme	Administering authority	Costs covered
Japan	Aid for modernising plant in SMEs	MITI	Aid to local bodies providing loans for plant modernisation in SMEs
	Special tax deduction for purchase of electronic equipment	Central government	Cost of specified small items of office machinery
	Special depreciation allowance for SMEs using certain office machines	Central government	Purchase of specified small items of office machinery
Portugal	New high-tech SMEs	Central government	Start-up costs
	Support for small investment projects	Central government	Start-up, development and modernisation of firms

2. Programmes dealing with the transfer of information

Country	Programme	Administering authority	Costs covered
Germany	Assistance for counselling in the sphere of energy saving	BMWi	Contribution to cost of services provided by special agencies
	Measures in support of SMEs	BMFi	Contribution to start-up consultancy costs
Australia	National Industry Extension Service (NIES)	Commonwealth Government States and Territories	Subsidies for services, information, analysis and counsel
Spain	Aid for commercial development	Ministry for Industry and Energy	Promotion and marketing costs (*e.g.* participation in trade fairs, congresses)
France	Aid for counselling and consultation	Regions	Contribution to cost of outside consultancy services
Japan	Aid for counselling	MITI	Contribution to cost of technological aid agency services
	Structural improvement	Public institutes	Advice and loans for counselling services
Norway	Subsidies awarded to National Institute of Technology	Central government	Transfer of information to enterprises
	Information services	Central government	Aid for transfer of new services and know-how to enterprises
United Kingdom	Design, quality, productivity, etc., counselling services	DTI	Contribution to cost of counselling services
Netherlands	Aid for information on management and for administrative information	Central government	Contribution to cost of management guidance services

Table 18. **Examples of support programmes for transferring technology resources to SMEs in various OECD countries, 1986-89** *(cont'd)*

Country	Programme	Administering authority	Costs covered
3. Programmes aimed at the players involved			
Japan	Assistance with organisation	MITI	Cost of help provided by National Federation of SME Associations and local bodies in organisation and training fields
	Assistance for counselling in management and technical skills	MITI	Cost of help provided by industrial and trade associations
United Kingdom	Management training		Cost of training managers

Source: OECD Industry Committee. Database on Subsidies and Industrial Adjustment.

projects were found to be highly innovative and the funding additional (on a scale of ratings). Sales and profit predictions were found to exceed the cost of the awards substantially, even allowing for optimism. Given the limited number of firms supported, the scheme was considered to be worthwhile and effective, and to have achieved the desired economic impacts.

Another UK programme that aimed at small firms (under 500 employees) – PDAC – involved design consultancy. It provided support to selected firms for innovation at the product design stage rather than the R&D stages. The scheme assisted companies at regional Product Design Advice Centres managed by the UK Design Council and, as it was experimental, evaluation was performed at an early stage. Each firm selected received 33 days' consulting for design and ten for marketing and finance. The scheme lasted for one year only (it was not renewed) and cost £1 million. The assessment was positive and there were indirect benefits.[23]

Impact evaluation took as its starting point the expectations of the firms, which were highly committed to a rapid development project that had business plans and consultancy specifications prepared in advance. Six months after the end of the scheme, of the 17 companies visited, four products were on the market; six were on field trials, in prototype or awaiting approval from outside agencies; three were awaiting the installation of manufacturing facilities; and four had not been developed significantly beyond the original concept. Impacts in terms of improvements in turnover, profit or employment were not considered valid to measure, given the early stage of evaluation.

The PDAC scheme provided indirect benefits: the increased confidence of firms in their own expertise and chosen solution; their introduction to new aspects of a technical field; and a more positive approach to the constructive use of consultants. Additionality was found: case-study companies stated that their projects would otherwise have been abandoned or taken place only with considerable delay. None of the projects from rejected companies were pursued. Supported companies would have been willing to contribute to the costs of the consultancy, and so the 100 per cent subsidy was higher than necessary.

Most of the firms assisted in the UK VANGUARD programme were SMEs with little knowledge of VADS. The scheme was relatively expensive to administer. In terms of impacts, it appeared that most of the firms participating in the initial phase had experienced increasing involvement and interest in VADS, but it was not possible to attribute this impact to the initiative. Most respondents said that the awareness scheme had demonstrated to them that investment in VADs was inappropriate at that time. This is a good example of a ''non-impact'' which is important (but not apparent from looking at statistics) and a beneficial outcome of the scheme. The impact of the second stage of the scheme (literature) was examined in terms of user opinion regarding usefulness; no impact could be measured. The evaluation concluded that awareness initiatives need real-time evaluation, as impacts quickly fade and are forgotten (making attribution very difficult). The stimulation of awareness does not necessarily result in measurable activity within a specified length of time.

For Germany, Meyer-Krahmer (1987 and 1990) has made an overall assessment of government programmes to support technology in SMEs during the late 1970s and early 1980s, comparing different programmes and instruments (direct and indirect – the latter essentially subsidies to R&D personnel). To a great extent, programmes of all types were most used by those SMEs that were already active in R&D (see Table 19).

For indirect programmes (R&D personnel subsidies), he judges that ''some 60 per cent of the funding volume was used for additional R&D and innovative activities''. This is relatively high in relation to additionality with fiscal programmes in Canada, the United States and Sweden. However, the rate of subsidy (40 per cent of gross salary costs) was high.

Meyer-Krahmer also considers the extent to which indirect government R&D programmes for SMEs have a spillover/externality effect on the innovation climate in firms, apart from the direct financial effect on participants profitability. Several studies had suggested that German programmes produce this effect by raising the visibility of R&D in general among SMEs and by strengthening the position of motivated people within firms. His conclusion, again, is that this (amplification) effect is only present in firms which are already actively engaged. There were no ''Sleeping Beauties''.

If indirect programmes have had, at best, an amplifying effect, have targeted programmes had more direct ''prime moving'' effects, shifting SMEs into ''first launches of major, more risky R&D projects or ventures into new sectors of technology''? To some extent the answer is yes but: *i)* only a very small number of (already active) firms have been involved; and *ii)* success has been technological rather than commercial, especially in relation to international competition.

The balance of BMFT support for SMEs shifted dramatically from direct (technology-specific) to indirect (non-selective) programmes. (The direct/indirect ratio shifted from 14.4:1 in 1976 to 2.4:1 in 1984).

Table 19. Technology-specific funding and R&D personnel grants in Germany

Evaluation criterion	Type of incentive	
	Technology-specific project funding (SMEs only)	R&D personnel grants
Support strategies		
– Goals	a) Supporting high technology to reach international level b) Balancing technology-specific deficits	a) General improvement of R&D potential b) Balancing general deficits of SMEs
– Selectivity	Very high	Very low
– Concentration on branches, regions	R&D-intensity dominates	R&D-intensity dominates
Clients		
– Degree of participation	Very limited	Very broad
– Innovativeness	Medium to high	Low to high, but mostly low
– Typical R&D projects	Relatively high-risk, costly, longer-term	Mostly small projects close to market
Effects on R&D		
– Share of high-risk, expensive and longer-term R&D projects	Large	Small
– Better R&D orientation	Clearly positive	Mainly in firms with existing technology
Effects on innovation and competitiveness		
– Time to commercial application	Long (esp. for SMEs)	Short
– First launch of major high-risk projects	Relatively frequent	Non existent
– Venturing into new areas of technology	Frequent	Rare
– Influence on accelerated structural change	Occasional	Diffuse
– Secondary effect: follow-on projects	Often large	Differing, limited
Effects on balancing innovation deficits financing	Very few firms have grave financial deficits	Very few firms have grave financial deficits
Administration		
– Barriers to access, especially for first-time applicants	High	Low (only manufacturing)
– Transparency of different possibilities	Low	Good
– Costs of application and administration	Large, absolute and relative	Medium
– Control	Large	Small
– Consulting	Administrative and technical available	Administrative: low, technical: none
Amount of grant	High	Lower, both absolutely and relatively
– Certainty of multi-annual funding	Longer lead time, then stable	Uncertainty about future funding

Source: Adapted from Meyer-Krahmer, 1987.

The BMFT provided DM 326 million to subsidise the application of computer-aided design and manufacture as part of its Production Technology Programme (1984-86). Firms received up to 40 per cent of costs for development work, including staff hardware/ software and external contracts in consultancy, R&D and training.

US support under the Small Business Innovation Research (SBIR) programme since 1982 is reviewed in NAS, NAE and IOM (1992) and Branscomb (1993). The conclusions are generally favourable to the programme, but not specific.

"SBIR was established in 1982 to fund SME R&D to stimulate the commercialisation of new products and processes. The programme also provides managerial and technical advice. The eleven federal agencies participating in the programme set aside 1.25 per cent of their research budgets each year to fund SBIR projects. The SBIR programme made 3 183 awards, valued at US$460 million, in fiscal year (FY) 1990. Grants were concentrated in the biotechnology field, energy systems, and defence-related projects. This programme has proved important in facilitating pre-commercial R&D in biotechnology, as well as providing a bridge across which companies can move from start-up to commercialisation." (NAS, NAE and IOM, 1992).

A much more critical assessment was made by Roessner, who judged that in spite of institutional evaluation requirements and procedures, "there is... little demand for a full, summative evaluation of SBIR. Those in a position to influence the programme do not want to consider eliminating it in favour of some as yet unknown, potentially more effective alternative programme. They seek only to ensure that it is meeting the narrower needs of their individual constituencies" (1989*b*, p. 351).

University/industry programmes

University/industry links have been promoted in various government programmes. In value terms, they represent a very small part of government efforts to promote industrial technology. They are (inevitably) very diffuse and difficult to evaluate. One attempt to present and analyse the issues is contained in the Bureau of Industry Economics (1991) evaluation of the Australian National Teaching Company Scheme, which also draws on earlier OECD work (see also Alic *et al.*, 1992; OTA, 1991).

International programmes and issues

Most evaluation of international programmes has concerned European programmes, primarily those of the EC but also including the European Space Agency and EUREKA. For some purposes these can be considered as "national", in the sense that they seek to promote innovation and competitiveness within a geographical space. However, they raise issues about wider competition and collaboration, about the distribution of benefits within the geographical space, and about their relation to national programmes within the same territory.

EC programmes have been very extensively reviewed. The BETA (1993) evaluation of various EC BRITE and EURAM programmes suggests very positive results (summarised in Table 13), but raises important questions. The methodology for distinguishing direct and indirect effects and quantifying them is outlined in Chapter 3 above and Table 12. "Minimum" estimates suggest that in terms of value added, each dollar of EC support is yielding some US$10-13 of direct benefit and some US$3-4 of indirect benefit.

However, the direct effects occurred in less than one-third of the firms participating, and almost 60 per cent of direct effects were located in 19 participants (11 per cent), all of which transferred applied mathematics from universities. Thus, in terms of direct effects, the EC R&D succeeded with a few winners and very many losers.

These results cannot easily be compared to commercial or social returns to R&D investment, or to financial returns in general. It is equally difficult to relate them to research results on elasticities of productivity to R&D expenditures. However, given any plausible assumption about the future path of benefits, the implied social returns to this EC R&D investment are very high indeed. The authors conclude that current policy interest in shifting government R&D from fundamental to technological research is wrong. Almost all the direct effects came from incremental innovations involving fundamental research.

The indirect effects were very important – with a ratio of 1:3-4, they would probably in themselves have justified the overall EC investment – and were much more widely dispersed than the direct effects. Nearly 90 per cent of participants reported indirect effects. Importantly, however, the indirect effects were concentrated in the large firms which also had direct effects.

The BETA analysis addresses several further issues. First, it compares large and small firms participating in the programmes. Both direct and indirect effects were, again, largely concentrated in the large firms, where the ratio of the value of effects to EC funding was also much higher. However, on average, the returns to SMEs participating was more than satisfactory. Nevertheless, the SME benefits were concentrated in a few firms which hold both a technological and market niche. Even so, "as soon as a big firm enters the niche, the battle is lost" (BETA, 1993, p. 29). More generally, the report points to the financial weakness of SMEs – their ability to take the risk of the associated investment needed to exploit the EC grant – and finds that they lack the critical mass needed to "integrate the functions of producer, user and research-tester".

Second, in relation to networking, BETA found that (with one major exception) there was no advantage in being the prime contractor: benefits were much higher among the sub-contractors.

Third, the ratio of effects to EC funding was very positive for research centre (3.0) and university (2.0) participants. As might be expected, the effects mainly fell under the heading of workforce (competence and training), but also some were technological (new contracts) (see Table 12).

Fourth, on technological/scientific success and failure, BETA assessed a sample of 50 programmes and found that 38 were successful and 12 were failures. This broadly confirms an earlier, larger survey of BRITE/EURAM programmes which found a 72 per cent success rate. However, in terms of economic success, of the 38 technologically-successful programmes, while all had economic effects, only 20 had direct effects (commercialised products or processes). Interestingly, of the twelve technological failures, eleven nevertheless had positive indirect effects.

The BETA team further noted a perverse effect "in many cases of co-operative research. On one side the State or the group of States pushes firms to work together; on the other side competition and confidentiality block the process of information exchange necessary for establishing a research consortium. The result of this dilemma is, in some cases, selection by the firms of scientific/technological subjects which have the minimum chance of providing direct economic effects, and the only justification for the project will be the generation of indirect economic effects. To make this inevitable bias acceptable, the programme selectors and managers should optimise the different mechanisms which favour the generation of these indirect effects; some of the criteria for the enhancement of such mechanisms are given in this report:

- ensure that fundamental research is closely linked to each step of the innovation process;
- associate at least one university lab with each consortium;
- avoid consortia with only SMEs;
- select generic technologies; etc.'' (BETA, 1993, p. 33).

Fifth, programme participants were invited to situate their research along a spectrum from basic research through applied research to quality control. Most research appeared to have been applied. Reclassifying the responses in terms of upstream (including applied) and downstream, some 60 per cent of direct effects were downstream and the direct returns to EC investment were much higher than for upstream research. However, the upstream research generated much greater indirect effects, with a very high (5.0) ratio of effects to EC investment.

Sixth, the presence of a university or research laboratory in a programme consortium greatly increased both direct and indirect effects.

Seventh, both direct and indirect effects were much higher in integrated firms where "producers, users, and testers (researchers)" were under one roof, than in consortia programmes or loose alliances.

Eighth, large projects produced relatively less (especially indirect) effects than small.

Lastly, there was an attempt to assess country differences in the results. These were massive, but the authors caution against hasty conclusions. Nevertheless, they note:

i) UK firms were far more successful than others in achieving effects (the ratio was 49.5:1 for direct and 8.1:1 for indirect): this could be both conjunctural (UK national R&D funding was being restricted) and cultural (EC public funding was better integrated in UK firm activities, by contrast with, for example, France and Italy).

ii) Small country firms achieved negligible direct effects, but substantial indirect effects (still well below the United Kingdom, but significantly above Germany, France and Italy).

iii) Germany and the Netherlands provide an interesting contrast: Germany did well on direct effects, but poorly on indirect effects – participants seemed to have oriented the programmes downstream – while the Netherlands' results were the reverse.

Using the same methodology, but confining themselves to the indirect effects, the BETA team have analysed ESA programmes and space activities in Canada. The results are summarised in Table 14. As with the EC programmes, the ratio of indirect effects to government funding was around 3.0:1 (3.5:1 for Canadian programmes). As the table indicates, the indirect effects were primarily and increasingly technological. "Work factor" effects, essentially skill and qualification acquisition which is redeployed within firms, were also very important.

These positive results raise some questions:

i) The economic returns to government seem very high: could (indeed, why would) market failure be this great? What about transaction costs?

ii) How much was the high return due to the international nature of the programmes (*e.g.* bringing together international partners who were hitherto unaware of collaboration possibilities or unable to realise them)? Can/do national programmes achieve such positive returns?

iii) Targeting – the positive results, especially the direct returns in the BRITE/EURAM programmes which were not targeted, were very much concentrated among a few participants: could targeting have further increased the returns?

iv) On the other hand, since the overall returns were so high (including the indirect effects), should these programmes not be greatly expanded?

v) With returns so much higher than financial returns to risk investment in general, how are the rents appropriated by different programme participants (including governments)?

Recent EC collaborative programmes have tried to limit themselves to pre-competitive research, and have made the results widely available in the public domain (or at least to a wide network of collaborating R&D institutions). EUREKA programmes, which are more market-oriented, are concerned with promoting European industrial competitiveness, and pose different evaluation problems. However, relations between EC and EUREKA programmes are complex and overlapping (OECD, 1989*b*, pp. 132-136).

In the case of EUREKA, official finance is not the central purpose of the programme (which depends on national *ad hoc* decisions), but can be seen as seed finance. The evaluation panel judged that for most participants the availability of official finance had not been a determining factor in the collaborative research, except possibly in the initial planning phase. Dissemination of research results was not judged important by participants or the evaluation panel, and a majority of participants were concerned with limiting dissemination to programme partners.

Watkins (1991, p. 100) argues that "the true value of broad programmes like EUREKA and ESPRIT is more likely to lie in the expansion of technology communication channels" than in support for specific technologies. He emphasises the role of such programmes in promoting networking, especially among small firms and firms at different vertical stages "along the technology food chain", and with emerging technology "where networks may not yet be established". He cites various evaluation survey studies in support, and further argues p. 101) that the "umbrella-consortia organisation design of EUREKA and ESPRIT – collecting a large number of independent collaboration research agreements – reduces the traditional kinds of contracting transactions costs... without the necessity of market concentration". Established procedures under the programmes simplify the negotiation process for each new agreement, especially on "technology sharing" between partners. This conclusion is considerably more favourable than those of the EC BRITE/EURAM evaluation.

Laredo and Callon (1990) argue that EC programmes have been "additional", and differ from national programmes in France in that they have promoted certain kinds of national TENs (through "basic technological research"), which call into question traditional notions about links along the spectrum from basic to applied research. However, it is less clear from the report that the programmes have promoted European TENs rather than restructuring the existing French ones.

International collaboration may seem justified in technology areas for which there will be a clear need for international norms/standards when the technology becomes competitive. However, the important norms are typically established through international commercial competition after the pre-competitive R&D stage. The EUREKA evaluation panel found that participants were not much concerned with the possibility of the programme promoting international standardisation. Collaboration in technology programmes would still seem important, at least for smaller countries, but would be directed to one of the subsequently competing technologies.

As noted earlier, there is a trade-off between promoting national competitiveness and obtaining economies of scale in, and access to, international programmes – especially for smaller countries and certain types of technology. There are no easy answers in terms of defining a space for competition (near-market R&D) and one for co-operation (pre-competitive R&D). Most countries emphasise national competitiveness objectives. In the larger countries, most programmes restrict participation to "national" organisations, especially in the case of enterprises. Moreover, in some instances (e.g. Australia), the criteria for access stipulate that the programme should enhance national competitiveness.

International collaboration is justified when the minimum programme size is too large for individual countries (or the risks too great), when there are important risks and international externalities (especially some environmentally-clean technologies), or when there will be a clear need for international standards when technology becomes competitive. However, the important norms are typically established through international commercial competition after the pre-competitive R&D stage. Pre-competitive programmes are more easily justified than near-market programmes.

One issue concerns the distribution of benefits between programme participants. There is very little conclusive evidence from evaluation studies on this. Small, more technologically-backward countries may be disadvantaged (Tsipouri, 1991), but equally, it is argued that the European approach of promoting flexible R&D collaboration has, after a somewhat shaky start due to questions of national contributions and returns, developed an *à la carte* approach which satisfies natural aspirations of participants within efficient programmes (Watkins, 1991).

This conclusion is considerably more favourable than those of the EC BRITE/EURAM evaluation by Linne (1991, pp. 12-13), which was based on detailed surveying of industrial programme participants. The conclusions on impacts are fairly negative. Essentially, they recommend a "bottom-up" approach in selecting both firms and technologies to support, but greater EC financial participation (60 per cent), better targeting (support for core projects), and a relative shift from large to smaller firms.

Probably, the most detailed and analytically interesting evaluation of the impacts of EC programmes is that of Laredo and Callon (1990 for France). Based on some 80 interviews and a postal survey (with some 650 replies – more than 40 per cent), it addressed all the important EC R&D programmes in the 1983-88 period. The conclusions are surprising and important:

    i) EC programmes were pervasive and important in the French R&D system.

    ii) The type of research promoted was different from that promoted by normal French Government financing – for the authors, it opened new avenues for public/private R&D relationships.

    iii) In other ways, the research did not meet traditional market failure justifications for government intervention: research teams did not change their strategic research orientations, they did not take on more risky research, and appropriation was not a central issue.

    iv) The (essentially) positive results of EC intervention were to promote new configurations of public and private R&D around new methodologies which shift the discussion about basic and applied research.

    v) However, the analysis left doubts about how these new positive configurations could be set up permanently without establishing the participants as institutionalised clients of the EC.

Conclusions

What is the role of government support in national innovation systems?

This report has addressed the question of efficiency with regard to government intervention to support national technology programmes; its focus is on the insertion of public programmes in national innovation systems and their effects on national competitiveness.

There have been various econometric studies (economy-wide, sectorial, microeconomic) of economic returns to R&D, and in some cases to government R&D; they are generally very positive on the overall returns to R&D, but fairly inconclusive on the role of government R&D. Other econometric studies (at different levels of aggregation) have examined the extent to which government R&D complements or substitutes for enterprise R&D. These have produced very mixed results but, on balance, suggest complementarity and additionality from government support. Clearly, econometric analysis should be taken further.

Quantitative (generally econometric) analysis has a part to play in the evaluation of national programmes. It can address some of the wider issues, including the effects of raising aggregate R&D levels and spillovers of innovation from sector to sector. However, it does not easily lend itself to the evaluation of specific programmes, except perhaps with broad indirect ones. Most importantly, it cannot really be used to investigate the role of government intervention.

Most of the discussion here centres on the more direct evaluation of specific programmes. Earlier sections have raised issues concerning objectives in identifiable programmes, justification for government intervention, different types of government programmes and the constraints of evaluation practice. The report stresses that there is considerable uncertainty in evaluating longer-term impacts, and that the problem of evaluation bias is a very real one.

National programmes that can be identified and evaluated for their impacts represent only a small part of government efforts to promote technology innovation and diffusion. Nevertheless, much of this support has economic implications which are, more or less, explicit objectives of specific programmes.

Governments need justification for support programmes. Much of the published discussion is about public accountability. (Did the programme achieve its stated objectives? Was it cost-efficient?) However, there is increasing concern about macroeconomic issues at a time when overall government budgets are constrained (see Table 15). Deadweight costs are significant.

The traditional neo-classical justifications for government intervention concern "market failure" – risks, externalities and minimum critical mass.

Wider (*e.g.* TEP) considerations suggest other justifications for government intervention – new growth theories, technology trajectories, promotion of "healthy" national innovation systems and globalisation. Recent analysis challenges linear notions of innovation and technology development/diffusion, or at least calls for a differentiation between types of technology and industry. In particular, it challenges the notion of precompetitive versus near-market research, with the implication that government's role should be primarily pre-competitive. This is important for policy discussions of what is acceptable/negotiable in the way of government support for R&D. More importantly, it raises issues about the extent to which innovation is/should be "demand-driven", and the resulting role for governments (promoting innovation in general or targeting markets/products/processes).

Governments have various – sometimes conflicting – objectives in supporting technology. Most government support is not primarily about economic objectives; it concerns national defence, public health, national education, the environment: technology for "public goods". The justification discussion raises questions:

  i) Justifications are permissive – to what extent should there be tighter criteria and "rules of the game"?
  ii) Doubts about linear notions of the innovation process call in question the distinction between pre-competitive and near-market R&D – how important is this in the justification of government intervention?

Public funding of technology development is only one of the possible policy responses to market failure. All the possible responses are conditioned by the reality of global oligopolistic competition and by the specificities of national innovation systems. The central problems remain: what did governments actually achieve? What would have happened without government intervention? How far would "free-riding" have been a more effective policy?

Evaluation issues with specific national programmes

Assessment of impacts is constrained by the very process of evaluation. "Arm's-length" evaluation, with independent and (if necessary) "second-guessing" of costs and outcomes, seems the most valid method; however, it is relatively costly, and the results may not easily be absorbed into policy discussions.

Given the above considerations, identifiable R&D programmes are very difficult to evaluate. The central problem is to identify impacts which are relevant both to programme objectives and to the wider policy concerns. Beyond this is the problem of relating these results to overall government efforts to support technology and national innovation systems.

Data availability is central. Most of the relevant impacts data are not in the public domain, but can only come from the willing collaboration of programme participants – hence, the importance of "institutionalising" the evaluation process. Better institutionalisation should lead to more data on more programmes in the public domain. At the very least, better institutionalisation could lead to greater transparency and wider coverage of evaluation in relation to overall government efforts to support technology. There may be interest in "meta-evaluation" of the evaluation process; this could include both the development of internationally-accepted criteria and a framework for individual evaluations, and further analysis of existing evaluations to make them internationally more comparable.

The need for greater transparency is especially important in relation to procurement. OECD's Data Base on Industrial Support Programmes activity is one approach: how much further can it be developed and exploited in relation to technology programmes? More work could be done on the net costs to government and to programme participants.

Different national approaches to technology policies and programmes are an important factor, but are embedded in historical political developments. They could be documented in terms of programme objectives and institutional mechanisms, but there is very little evidence on the outcomes. Moreover, as the report indeed stresses, identifiable/ assessable programmes represent only a part of government efforts to support technology, while the lives of individual programmes are very much influenced by exogenous events. Nevertheless, there is interest in further comparative analysis between countries of specific programmes which have comparable objectives. Comparability could include: the type of instrument (*e.g.* fiscal measures), a specific technology (with a trajectory) and sector (*e.g.* an alternative energy), and the diffusion process (SMEs, national laboratory-enterprise links).

The impacts data required for evaluation of the wider technology concerns are necessarily longer-term; therefore, there is a need for intermediate indicators. Some work is under way on these (*e.g.* patents, bibliometrics); the experience so far is not encouraging. Moreover, there are formidable problems with using them to evaluate government technology support. Governments are justified in intervening primarily because there is market failure (*i.e.* not a typical situation) and their objectives (*e.g.* in terms of intellectual property rights) may be different from those of other programme participants.

Most efforts have involved surveying *i)* programme participants, on what they have done and on their expectations, and *ii)* non-participants, on why they did not participate and (rarely) on how the programme nevertheless affected their activities. In formal statistical terms, the results have varied in their significance. The more intractable problem has been motivating responses to surveys, and the formulation of questions. In spite of the efforts of the researchers, there could be suspicions of optimism/loyalty in the results.

"Arm's-length" *ex post* investigative evaluation has played an important role, but has necessarily been concerned with individual large programmes whose results have moved (extremely slowly) towards the public domain. These programmes are not necessarily representative – and are also expensive in research terms.

Raising overall R&D efforts

Indirect government programmes to support R&D are pervasive in the OECD Member countries. Importantly, they include government procurement and equity participation, which have been largely excluded from policy analysis because their impacts are very difficult to assess. There is no evidence that allows an overall assessment of the share of different government instruments in support of technology and R&D. Procurement is probably the most important, but it is the least well documented and not included in most statements or analysis of specific programmes. Most of the analysis and policy discussion is about fiscal support.

Fiscal supports to private R&D are widespread throughout OECD countries and are generally embedded in national fiscal systems. In addition, there have been specific programmes to support industrial R&D. In some countries, they represent an important share of overall government efforts to support R&D. The evidence on these programmes is fairly inconclusive, but probably on balance positive. First, analysis of the ratio of induced R&D to foregone government revenue has yielded very divergent results (from 0.3-0.4, which is worryingly low, to 2.0, which would seem to be very high). However, there are large differences between sectors/technologies and types of firm. The major problems for enterprises concern expectations about their tax situation and about the stability of programmes. Second, how much can this induced R&D be assimilated to other enterprise R&D in terms of its impacts? In general, there is massive evidence that social returns are higher than private returns, but to what extent is this true for government-induced R&D?

Economic evaluation of specific programmes

Economic evaluation of impacts is problematic, and not adequately covered in most formal evaluations. In cost/benefit terms, the difficulty is mainly in evaluating the benefits. Longer-term impacts are also difficult for all their uncertainties, and evaluation bias can be daunting. Meanwhile, the real costs of government R&D programmes are considerable – perhaps twice the nominal costs, although considerably lower in indirect programmes.

"National competitiveness" is a particularly tricky criterion of success in evaluating specific national programmes. Where it was relevant, most evaluations – based on survey participant responses – have concluded that the national programme would lead to significant benefits, justifying the programme. In a few cases, the question of involving multinational enterprises in the national programme has been considered.

This report emphasises the problem of risk in more or less targeted programmes. R&D is inherently risky for both technical and commercial reasons. Governments are justified in taking more risks than programme participants for portfolio reasons. However, in some countries, overall government efforts have been dominated by very few programmes. Moreover, in economic terms, the "returns" to a programme need to include the failures as well as the successes, and these are not well represented in available evaluation reports.

An important issue concerns the allocation of benefits to the government intervention. Most of the costs of bringing a product or process to successful commercialisation are incurred after the R&D phase, and the success of commercialisation depends on decisions/events which are beyond the scope of the official intervention. The evidence on impacts that can be clearly allocated to government intervention is inconclusive, although most overall evaluations are on balance positive. However, any assessment of commercial or "near-market" outcomes seems to run rapidly into problems of commercial confidentiality.

The report raises the complex issues of technology appropriation and the innovation system. Non-appropriability of the results of R&D activities is a major justification for government intervention to support R&D. Governments can seek to reduce the area of non-appropriability by granting protection through intellectual property rights, to widen the area of R&D results into the category of "public goods", or to deal with market failure by other means. Measures to correct for market failure therefore do not necessarily require government finance for R&D. With public support for R&D, there is an unresolved question about who should acquire the intellectual property rights and the resulting "economic rents". There are major empirical problems in analysing appropriability and intellectual property rights. Successful appropriation (*e.g.* measured by patenting) is not a good indicator of programme success. Not enough is known about how enterprises seek and use appropriation; how far is policy discussion useful? Are further empirical studies a priority?

Promotion of innovation

No overall assessment of the extent or effectiveness of targeting is possible, because this depends on administrative practice as much as on the stated objectives. Its "track record" is not good, but a very few winners may be worth many losers. However, in relation to this justification, evaluation should consider the whole programme portfolio, losers as well as winners. Most evaluations report significant successes, which largely justify government intervention. Some point to the catalyst role of government in bringing partners together and launching programmes.

With regard to targeting *versus* general support for R&D and technology:

  i) the available evidence offers mixed results – targeting of large programmes has had devastating failures (with implications outside the target areas) but probably some successes: there is no overall conclusion, but it would probably be negative; and governments have special difficulties in efficiently pursuing innovation beyond the "pre-competitive" stage;

  ii) targeting is now much more about generic/critical technologies – there is a different problem with new "demand-driven" priorities.

95

Targeting and generic technologies thus raise several policy issues:

  i) Does past experience suggest lessons/constraints in developing programmes for emerging technologies?

  ii) To what extent should countries develop national programmes or, alternatively, be free-riders?

  iii) How can wasteful competition be avoided?

  iv) What is the role of norms/standards?

National innovation systems and diffusion

Techno-economic networks play a crucial role in technology development and diffusion, and justify government intervention. However, they are not well captured in most evaluations of government programmes. What are the criteria for desirable and successful developments – convergence? stability? flexibility? The evidence is again somewhat inconclusive. There is considerable survey evidence that (particularly pre-competitive) programmes have promoted networking in collaborative R&D. Moreover, the establishment of collaborative partnerships can be clearly traced to the catalyst effect of establishing a government programme. However, there are key questions concerning the reliability of the evidence and the appropriateness and durability of the collaborations (*e.g.* commercial success).

As regards specific SME programmes, some [*e.g.* the US Small Business Innovation Research (SBIR) programme] report considerable success. German programmes have had general success, but the impacts have been heavily concentrated in a few firms which were already active in R&D: in other words, there is no general diffusion effect. The overall OECD (1993) assessment was fairly negative.

Indirect effects, *i.e.* externalities/spillovers from government programmes, seem central to overall assessment. Some evaluations accord them a priority high enough to justify government intervention without the direct effects. Most analysis, (including econometric) shows much more modest or inconclusive results. However, their evalua-tion poses formidable causality problems, and most of the relevant programmes were not primarily concerned with economic or national competitive objectives.

International issues

This report has attempted to situate national government efforts to support technol-ogy in relation to NIS. This is difficult, because *i)* they are only a part of NIS, and *ii)* they have other objectives – technology for public goods – that cannot easily be challenged internationally (*e.g.* as subsidies to industry). The focus has been on their economic impacts, including national competitiveness, in a world characterised by globalised oligo-polistic competition.

Thus, these efforts raise international policy issues, suggesting:

i) an area of competition, where governments seek directly or indirectly (through better use of their technology programmes for public goods) to enhance national competitiveness; here, the international policy issues are about transparency, and the level playing field and rules of the game (subsidies, etc.);

ii) an area of collaboration, where R&D is pre-competitive or the public goods are international or, more generally, where governments do not feel threatened immediately by international collaboration; this is a fairly fragile area, probably small in relation to overall government efforts, but probably worth international policy promotion.

There is a trade-off between promoting national competitiveness and obtaining economies of scale in, and access to, international programmes – especially for smaller countries and certain types of technology. There are no easy answers in terms of defining a space for competition (near-market R&D) and one for co-operation (pre-competitive R&D). International collaboration is justified when the minimum programme size is too large for individual countries (or the risks too great), or when the R&D is about international (*e.g.* environmental) problems. It has not always been efficient in terms of bringing products/processes to the market. Moreover, it has not always been a positive sum game, and OECD Member countries do not play it as though it were. Nevertheless, collaboration may frequently be the "least worst" strategy. Most evaluations of international collaborative programmes have found the outcomes successful in terms of promotion of technical results and international research collaboration. A few have raised questions about the distributive aspects. Who benefited most? Were "small" participants disfavoured? There may be a general trade-off between maximising programme coverage (networking) and programme efficiency.

Notes

1. The report, a preliminary overview, draws on material readily available to the Secretariat. Some information stems from earlier work sponsored by the OECD – and for the most part conducted within the Directorate for Science, Technology and Industry – which generated a network of contacts with national and international institutions concerned with the assessment of national technology programmes.

   An important workshop was held in December 1987 on the "Evaluation of Government Programmes Promoting Technological Innovation". The major contributions to this workshop have been published both by the OECD (1990*b*) and, in revised form, in a special issue of the journal *Research Policy* (Roessner, 1989*a*).

   Recently, the OECD developed an ongoing evaluation activity concerned with industrial subsidies and structural adjustment, which involves an Industrial Subsidies Data Base (DISP) based on Member country responses to an agreed questionnaire. The initial results (some 900 entries) are being evaluated for both their methodological significance and their completeness. At the present stage (OECD 1992*b*), these results cannot be used in detail for reasons of confidentiality, but the analysis represents an important input to the assessment of national technology programmes. It should be emphasised that its focus is very different from the present concerns: first, assessment of the subsidy element in government industrial policies is only one (albeit important) aspect of the evaluation of national technology programmes; secondly, subsidies to R&D activities are only a small, if increasing, part of total industrial subsidies. Moreover, it appears that the DISP has only captured a small part (about 20 per cent) of total government effort devoted to supporting industrial innovation activities (as recorded in the OECD STIID R&D activities). Nevertheless, the DISP has proved invaluable to the present report in pointing the way to individual programmes and assessing the different types of government intervention in the support of national technology programmes.

   In preparing its annual reviews of industrial policy (OECD, 1990*a* and 1991), the DSTI examines measures to promote R&D, innovation and technology diffusion. While these reviews are primarily concerned with current policy developments and are therefore not an exhaustive description (and not at all concerned with the evaluation of impacts), they are the best descriptive source.

   DSTI also completed work in 1992 on *Small and Medium-sized Enterprises (SMEs): Technology and Competitiveness* (OECD, 1993). Although this work does not really deal with the evaluation of impacts, the data and conclusions are used below, particularly in Chapter 4.

2. While TEP does not take sides on most of the outstanding issues, it does underline the need to reconcile neo-classical technology/economic concepts and analysis with a variety of recent analyses which point to different conclusions on technology and national competitiveness. Some of these ideas are reflected in current DSTI work on innovation surveys and codified in the Oslo Manual (OECD, 1992*c*).

3. It is not easy to judge the extent to which allocations for R&D are really for industrial development; there is a "labelling problem". One important Canadian programme is labelled as The Defence Industry Productivity Program, but in most discussion is considered to be government support for industrial development.

4. Folster (1988) proposes three slightly different criteria for government support for private R&D:
   - government should not finance a project that the firm would otherwise undertake;
   - the social value of the project should not be negative;
   - the subsidy should provide an incentive to maximise the project's social value.

5. However, Watkins (1991) argues that, in the presence of transaction costs, R&D results are "impure public goods". In this case, it may be a legitimate policy aim to promote R&D consortia (as in ESPRIT and EUREKA), and restrict the diffusion of their results to consortia participants.

6. Ergas (1993) argues that the French nuclear programme was relatively successful in adaptation, whereas UK programmes were much less successful. Cohen and Noll (1991) suggest that in the latter case, adapting to changing perceptions of risks and likely programme success was a major problem.

7. These issues are taken up, if not resolved, in a number of evaluations (see for example Linne, 1991 and Bureau of Industry Economics, 1991).

8. The DISP discussion within OECD suggested three broad types of R&D support programme: programmes aiming to increase enterprises' R&D expenditures in general – here, fiscal aids would be the main instrument; programmes supporting certain areas of R&D expenditures; and programmes to strengthen the R&D expenditures of certain categories of enterprises (region, size group). Moreover, the DISP does not seem to include most government support to its own research laboratories or, more generally, intramural government research (in the STIID sense). On the other hand, the DISP also does not identify the R&D expenditures of programmes for which R&D is not the primary cost to government. Thus, for all (879) DISP programmes taken as a whole, while R&D costs were predominant in 1989 for 12.6 per cent of total costs, a further 3.8 per cent was allocated to "specialised investment" (which, in some cases, had a major innovation component) and 2.5 per cent was allocated as support to non-profit organisations (some of which would be primarily R&D organisations – e.g. industry-specific R&D associations). In most of these cases, the instrument would be direct, essentially grants or loans.

9. Branscomb (1992) has argued that "the common-sense definition of 'precompetitive' is any kind of R&D that isn't proprietary. A more precise adjective would be 'not anticompetitive'. As a guide to policy, this is unacceptably broad. However, it does suggest one appropriate role for government to support R&D that underpins a broad array of specific technology applications in many different industries, while stopping short of supporting proprietary technology that companies themselves should fund".

10. It should be noted that this analysis concerns only "direct" programmes, essentially enterprise R&D financed or contracted by federal agencies. "Indirect" programmes seem relatively important in Canada.

11. For a general methodological discussion, see Cordes (1989). For a summary of OECD corporate income tax treatment of R&D, see OECD (1988).

12. According to the DISP data, very few loans seem to have been repaid during the period covered. However, from an evaluation point of view, this does not necessarily mean that the loan programmes were unsuccessful in terms of their objectives. Apart from the inevitable

reluctance of recipients to repay and the difficulty of checking individual loans, the time horizon for achieving profitable results may be well beyond the corresponding accounting or fiscal horizon. In any case, major loan repayments in the limited period covered by the DISP are unlikely. One estimate suggests that roughly 25 per cent of Swedish STU loans are repaid (Folster, 1988).

13. This is a "residual" calculation which comes from comparing two different sets of statistics. For a general review, see, for example, Branscomb (1993) and Toulemonde (1990). For analysis of some well-known examples, see Cohen and Noll (1991); Ergas (1987 and 1993); Henderson (1977); and Palda (1992).

14. Inevitably, most of the survey evidence is about participants' attitudes to the programmes and their management and collaborative aspects. However, much of this evidence is "suspect" from an impacts point of view: dissatisfied firms may not respond, and those that do (strictly speaking, the individuals that respond) may feel motivated to respond positively. There is rather little in the evaluation literature about these response issues.

15. One difficult problem in cost/benefit analysis concerns what prices to use. There is a strong case for using expected international prices for both costs and (even more so) benefits. If domestic market prices and exchange rates do not reflect the real opportunity costs to the national economy, the cost/benefit results may be biased. In particular, the presence of large policy-induced price distortions through protection and subsidies (including the R&D programme) may lead to significant overstatement of benefits if market prices are used. In one CSIRO case evaluated (the CDT pulse welder), the benefit/cost ratio fell from 2.2 with market prices to 1.6 using international prices.

The decision to use domestic prices in most evaluations has been implicit and practical; essentially, that evaluation is part of an institutionalised process which needs to be acceptable to programme participants. In the Brookings case, it was explicit: the analysis sought to simulate what would have been the relevance of cost/benefit analysis to programme sponsors and participants using the expected prices during the lifetime of the programmes.

16. See Alic et al. (1992, p. 61) for a list of nine potential criteria for evaluation. Their conclusions p. 64) are cautionary: "Which of the above standards of comparison is the 'right' one? It is the one that matches the public policy alternative being proposed. Analysis and policy must go together: blanket assessments of the 'value' of spin-off, pro or con, are rarely relevant to actual policy choices. Even when a specific approach, hence a particular standard can be identified, evaluation is not straightforward. Many of the comparisons summarised here have been debated at least implicitly in the literature, but the results have remained inconclusive. Policies have not been tested on a scale sufficient for valid conclusions, and testing by means of analytic models has remained generally beyond the capability of modern econometric techniques."

17. "Prior to the introduction of the 150 per cent tax concession for R&D, business enterprise expenditures on R&D (BERD) were increasing rapidly following a period of very slow growth. Following the introduction of the concession, private BERD accelerated: ABS estimate that nominal expenditures increased by 28 per cent in 1985-86 and by 29 per cent in 1986-87. From the BIE's survey it was clear that expenditures on R&D by those firms registering for the concession increased at a more rapid rate; 82 per cent in 1985-86 and 31 per cent in 1986-87. Furthermore, respondents reported that concessional R&D increased at four times the rate of non-concessional R&D in 1986-87" (Bureau of Industry Economics, 1989). Mansfield (1986) suggests that creative accounting and reclassification is unlikely to lead to an overestimation of more than 14 per cent.

18. "While some substitution of concessional R&D, and some reclassification of expenditures as R&D may have occurred, these observations attest to the positive role that the concession has had in promoting R&D. However, this large increase in R&D cannot be attributed to the tax concession alone. Other factors identified and measured included the cost of conducting R&D, changed accounting and reporting procedures, and natural growth... Companies indicated that around 17 per cent of the nominal increase in R&D was due to the tax concession. That is, around 32 per cent of the real increase in R&D was due to the tax concession. This is further evidence that the concession did have an impact at the margin" (Bureau of Industry Economics, 1989).

19. "It is not possible to make a strict comparison between the impact of the tax concession on R&D and the revenues foregone. The Bureau's survey of concession registrants covered around three-quarters of the increase in private BERD between 1984-85 and 1986-87 (A$ 313 million out of A$ 426 million), and around 17 per cent of this increase was attributed to the tax concession by respondents to the BIE's survey. Given the estimated cost of the concession of A$ 316 million during this period, the ratio of revenues foregone to the increase in private BERD was possible in the region of 4:1 for these years" (Bureau of Industry Economics, 1989).

20. "Such a result is to be expected and does not necessarily mean that the tax concession is cost-ineffective.
First, no scheme can guarantee a short-run increase in R&D equivalent to the revenues foregone. A specific grants scheme which provides subsidies for individual projects will, like a tax concession, almost certainly fund projects which would have gone ahead without government assistance. The concession was seeking to permanently raise business R&D, through a process of attitudinal change, rather than to fund a temporary increase in R&D performance. The relevant comparison cannot therefore be made in the short term, but must await some time until attitudinal changes become obvious. Second, administrative difficulties, which are in the process of being overcome, are likely to have reduced the short-term impact of the concession. Thirdly, the present day costs of the concession in terms of revenue are not known – but because of the changes to taxation arrangements... they are likely to be much less than previously estimated. Fourth, the value of the concession will be the increase in innovation which results from the R&D, rather than the expenditure on R&D itself" (Bureau of Industry Economics, 1989).

21. There is no way of knowing how representative this sample was.

22. The analysis gives no data on the 30 projects evaluated. It is an exploration of possible outcomes, with a wide range of programme variables.

23. The evaluation was carried out by a university team on behalf of DTI and concentrated on impacts and appropriateness; it involved interviews with firms, centre managers, Design Council staff and design consultants. Failed applicants were included in the interview sample.

Bibliography

ALIC, John A., Lewis M. BRANSCOMB, Harvey BROOKS, Ashton B. CARTER and Gerald L. EPSTEIN (1992), *Beyond Spin-off: Military and Commercial Technologies in a Changing World,* Harvard Business School Press.

ALVEY (1991), *Evaluation of the Alvey Programme for Advanced Information Technology,* HMSO, London.

AMABLE, Bruno and Robert BOYER, "The R&D Productivity Relationship in the Context of New Growth Theories: Some Recent Applied Research", in Capron (ed.), *Proceedings of the Workshop on Quantitative Evaluation of the Impact of R&D Programmes,* EC MONITOR/ SPEAR Programme, EUR 14.740 EN.

ATKINSON, R.D. (1991), "Innovation Policy Making in a Federalist System: Lessons from the States for US Federal Innovation Policy Making", *Research Policy 20.*

AUDITOR-GENERAL (1989), *Efficiency Audit Report on Taxation Concession and Grants for Industry Research and Development Schemes,* AGPS, Canberra.

AUDRETSCH, David B. and Hideki YAMAWAKI (1998), "R&D Rivalry, Industrial Policy, and US-Japanese Trade", *Review of Economics and Statistics,* Vol. LXX, No 3.

BACH, L. and G. LAMBERT (1993), "Evaluation of the Economic Effects of Large R&D Programmes: the Case of the European Space Programme", *Research Evaluation.*

BACH, L., P. COHENDET, G. LAMBERT and M.J. LEDOUX (1992), "Measuring and Managing Spin-offs: The Case of the Spin-offs Generated by ESA Programs" *Space Economics,* Vol. 144, pp. 171-206, American Institute of Aeronautics and Astronautics, Washington, DC.

BARBARIE, A. (1990), "Evaluation of Programmes Promoting Technological Innovation in Canada" in *OECD Public Management Studies,* No. 6, Paris.

BERNSTEIN, Jeffrey I. and M. Ishaq NADIRI (1991), "Product Demand, Cost of Production, Spillovers, and the Social Rate of Return to R&D", NBER Working Paper No. 3625.

BETA (Bureau d'économie théorique et appliquée) (1988), *Étude sur les effets économiques des dépenses spatiales européennes, Vol. I: Résultats, Vol. II: Rapport théorique et méthodologique,* Université Louis-Pasteur, Strasbourg.

BETA (Bureau d'économie théorique et appliquée) (1993), *Economic Evaluation of the Effects of the BRITE-EURAM Programmes on the European Industry: Final Report,* Université Louis-Pasteur, Strasbourg.

BOBE, B. (1991), "Trends in the Use of R&D Output Indicators in EC Programme Evaluation", *Scientometrics,* July-August.

BRANSCOMB, Lewis M. (1992), "Does America Need a Technology Policy?", *Harvard Business Review,* March-April.

BRANSCOMB, Lewis M. (ed.) (1993), *Empowering Technology: Implementing a US Strategy*, MIT Press.

BRANSCOMB, Lewis M. (1994), "Targeting Critical Technologies", *STI Review*, No. 14, OECD, Paris.

BROWN, Marilyn A., Linda G. BERRY and Rajeev K. GOEL (1991), "Guidelines for Successfully Transferring Government-sponsored Innovations", *Research Policy 20*, pp. 121-143.

BUREAU OF INDUSTRY ECONOMICS (1989), *The 150% Tax Concession for Research and Development Expenditure*, Interim Report, Australian Government Publishing Service.

BUREAU OF INDUSTRY ECONOMICS (1991), *The National Teaching Company Scheme*, Australian Government Publishing Service.

BUREAU OF INDUSTRY ECONOMICS (1992), *Economic Evaluation of CSIRO Industrial Research*, Australian Government Publishing Service.

BUREAU OF INDUSTRY ECONOMICS (1993), "R&D, Innovation and Competitiveness: An Evaluation of the Research and Development Tax Concession", Research Report 50, Canberra.

CALLON, M., P. LAREDO and V. RABEHARISOA (1991), "Des instruments pour la gestion et l'évaluation des programmes technologiques: le cas de l'AFME", in De Bandt and Foray (eds.), *L'Évaluation économique de la recherche et du changement technique*, CNRS, Paris.

CALLON, M., P. LAREDO and V. RABEHARISOA (with T. GONARD and T. LERAY) (1992), "The Management and Evaluation of Technological Programmes and the Dynamics of Techno-Economic Networks: The Case of AFME", *Research Policy 21*, pp. 215-236.

CAPRON, Henri (1992), *Economic Quantitative Methods for the Evaluation of R&D Programmes: A State of the Art*, EC MONITOR-SPEAR Programme, EUR 14.864 EN.

CAPRON, Henri (1993), "The Applied Econometrics of R&D Public Funding: What's That For?" in Capron (ed.), *Proceedings of the Workshop on Quantitative Evaluation of the Impact of R&D Programmes*, EC MONITOR/SPEAR Programme, EUR 14.740 EN.

CAPRON, Henri and Olivier DEBANDE (1993), "Designing Efficient R&D Policies in a Competitive Environment: What about the Strategic Issues", in Capron (ed.), *Proceedings of the Workshop on Quantitative Evaluation of the Impact of R&D Programmes*, EC MONITOR/SPEAR Programme, EUR 14.740 EN.

CHABBAL, R. (1987), *Organisation of Research Evaluation in the CEC*, European Community, Brussels, November.

CNER (1992), *Évaluation du programme spatial français*, Paris.

COHEN, Linda R. and Roger G. NOLL (1991), *The Technology Pork Barrel*, Brookings Institution.

CORDES, Joseph J. (1989), "Tax Incentives and R&D Spending: A Review of the Evidence", *Research Policy 18*, pp. 119-133.

DE BANDT, J. and D. FORAY (eds.) (1991), *L'Évaluation économique de la recherche et du changement technique*, Éditions du CNRS, Paris.

DITC (1991*a*), *Review of the Communications Technology Component of the Generic Technology Grants Scheme*, Information Industries Branch, DITC, May.

DITC (1991*b*), *Review of the Biotechnology Component of the Generic Technology Grant Scheme*, DITC, Canberra, September.

EC (1991), *Patents as Indicators of the Utility of European Community R&D Programmes*, EC MONITOR/SPEAR Programme, EUR 13.661 EN.

ERGAS, H. (1987), "Does Technology Policy Matter?" in B.R. Guile and H. Brooks (eds.), *Technology and Global Industry,* National Academy Press, Washington, DC.

ERGAS, H. (1993), "A Future for Mission-oriented Policies? A Critical Review of Developments in Europe", *Futures* (forthcoming).

EUREKA (1991), *The Report of the EUREKA Assessment Panel.*

FOLSTER, S. (1988), "The 'Incentive Subsidy' for Government Support of Private R&D", *Research Policy 17,* pp. 105-112.

GAO (1991), *Diffusing Innovations: Implementing the Technology Transfer Act of 1986,* Government Accounting Office, Programme Evaluation and Methodology Division.

GRILICHES, Z. (1990), "The Search for R&D Spillovers", Working Paper, Harvard University, Cambridge.

GRUPP, H., U. SCHMOCH and U. KUNTZE (1991), "Patents as Potential Indicators of the Utility of EC Research Programmes", *Scientometrics,* Vol. 21, No. 3, pp. 417-445.

GUMMETT, P. (1992), "Civil and Military Aircraft in the UK", *History and Technology,* Vol. 9, pp. 203-222.

HALL, Bronwyn H. (1992), "R&D Tax Policy during the Eighties: Success or Failure?", *NBER Working Paper No. 4240.*

HANEL, P. and K. PALDA (1992), "Appropriability and Public Support of R&D in Canada", paper contributed to INSEE seminar on "L'Appropriation technologique", Paris.

HEATON, G.R., R. REPETTO and R. SOBIN (1992), *Backs to the Future: US Government Policy toward Environmentally Critical Technology,* World Resources Institute, June.

HENDERSON, P.D. (1977), "Two British Errors: Their Probable Size and Some Possible Lessons", *Oxford Economic Papers,* Vol. 29, No. 2.

ISNOR, Richard (1993), "Federal Biotechnology Policy in Canada: Relative Success or Ineffectiveness" in *Science and Public Policy,* Vol. 20, No. 1.

IRVING, Clive (1993), *Wide-Body: The Making of the 747,* Hodder & Stoughton.

JACQUEMIN, Alexis (1988), "Co-operative Agreements in R&D and European Antitrust Policy", *European Economic Review 32,* No. 2/3, pp. 551-560, North Holland.

KRULL, W., D. SENSI and D. SOTIRIOU (1991), *Evaluation of R&D: Current Practice and Guidelines,* EUR 13.336 EN.

LAREDO, P. and M. CALLON (1990), *L'impact des programmes communautaires sur le tissu scientifique et technique français,* ministère de la Recherche et de la Technologie, Paris, January.

LEVIN, Richard C., Alvin K. KLEVORICK, Richard C. NELSON and Sidney G. WINTER (1987), "Appropriating the Returns from Industrial R&D", *Brookings Papers on Economic Activity,* No. 3.

LEVY, D. (1990), "Estimating the Impact of Government R&D", *Economic Letters,* Vol. 32 (2), pp. 169-173.

LICHTENBERG, F. (1987), "The Effect of Government Funding on Private Industrial Research and Development: A Re-Assessment", *Journal of Industrial Economics,* 36[1], pp. 97-104.

LINNE, H. (1991), *Key Factors for Industrial Partnership in EC Programmes,* EUR 13.991, CEC, Brussels.

MAIRESSE, J. and M. SASSENOU (1991a), "R&D and Productivity: A Survey of Econometric Studies at the Firm Level", *STI Review,* No. 8, OECD, Paris.

MAIRESSE, J. and M. SASSENOU (1991b), "Recherche-développement et productivité: un panorama des études économetriques sur données d'entreprises" in De Bandt and Foray (eds.), *L'Évaluation économique de la recherche et du changement technique,* CNRS, Paris.

MANSFIELD, E. (1986), "The R&D Tax Credit and Other Technology Policy Issues", *American Economic Review,* Vol. 76, pp. 190-194.

MASSIMO, L. (1991), "The Use of Indicators in the R&D Evaluation Activity of the European Communities", *Scientometrics,* July-August.

McKEON, R. and J.A. RYAN (1989), "Evaluation of Programs Promoting Technological Innovation: The Australian Experience", *Research Policy 18,* No. 6.

MEYER-KRAHMER, F. (1984), "Recent Results in Measuring Innovation Output", *Research Policy 13,* pp. 175-184.

MEYER-KRAHMER, F. (1987), "Evaluating Innovation Policies: The German Experience", *Technovation 5,* pp. 317-330.

MEYER-KRAHMER, F. (1990), "The Determinants of Investment in R&D and the Role of Public Policies: An Evaluation", in E. Deiaco, E. Hornell, and G. Vickery (eds.), *Technology and Investment,* Pinter Publishers, London, pp. 167-184.

MEYER-KRAHMER, F. and P. MONTIGNY (1989), "Evaluation of Innovation Programmes in Selected European Countries", *Research Policy 18,* pp. 313-332.

MOHNEN, P. (1991), "Survol de la littérature sur les externalités technologiques", in De Bandt and Foray (eds.), *L'Évaluation économique de la recherche et du changement technique,* CNRS, Paris.

MULLER, J. (1989), "Policy Options for Government Funding of Advanced Technology: The Case of International Collaboration in the European Telecommunication Satellite Programme", *Research Policy 18,* pp. 33-50.

NAS, NAE, and IOM, (1992), *The Government Role in Civilian Technology: Building a New Alliance,* National Academy Press, Washington, DC.

NATIONAL RESEARCH COUNCIL (1990), *Expanding Access to Precompetitive Research in the US and Japan: Biotechnology and Optoelectronics,* National Academy Press, Washington, DC.

NEA (1993), *Spin-off Technologies Developed through Nuclear Activities,* OECD, Paris.

OECD (1986), *Innovation Policy: France,* Paris.

OECD (1988), *Tax Reform and Industrial Performance,* Paris.

OECD (1989a), *OECD Science and Technology Indicators Report No. 3,* Paris.

OECD (1989b), *Major R&D Programmes for Information Technology,* Paris.

OECD (1990a), *Industrial Policy in OECD Countries, Annual Review,* Paris.

OECD (1990b), "Evaluation of Programmes Promoting Technological Innovation", *Public Management Studies No. 6,* Paris.

OECD (1990c), *Evaluation of Programmes Promoting Research, Technology and Innovation: Check-list of Principles,* Paris.

OECD (1991), *Industrial Policy in OECD Countries, Annual Review,* Paris.

OECD (1992a), *Technology and the Economy: The Key Relationships,* Paris.

OECD (1992b), "Industrial Support Policies in OECD: 1986-89", OCDE/GD(92)126, Paris.

OECD (1992c), "Proposed Guidelines for Collecting and Interpreting Technological Innovation Data: Oslo Manual", OCDE/GD(92)26, Paris.

OECD (1992d), *Technology and Productivity: The Challenge for Economic Policy,* Paris.

OECD (1993), *Small and Medium-sized Enterprises (SMEs): Technology and Competitiveness,* Paris.

OLDS, B.J. (1992), *Technological Eur-phoria? An Analysis of European Community Science & Technology Programme Evaluation Reports,* Netherlands Ministry of Economic Affairs.

ORMALA, E. (1989), "Nordic Experiences of the Evaluation of Technical R&D", *Research Policy 18,* pp. 333-342.

OTA (1991), *Federally Funded Research: Decisions for a Decade,* OTA-SET-491, April, Washington, DC.

PALDA, K. (1992), Draft of second edition of *Industrial Policy,* The Fraser Institute, Vancouver (1st edition: 1984).

QUO-TEC (1992), *Evaluation of BioResearch Ireland,* Final report to Department of Industry and Commerce.

ROESSNER, J.D. (ed.) (1989a), "Special Issue on Evaluation of Government Innovation Programs", *Research Policy 18,* No. 6.

ROESSNER, J.D. (1989b), "Evaluating Government Innovation Programs: Lessons from the US Experience", *Research Policy 18,* pp. 343-59.

ROMER, Paul M. (1993), "Implementing a National Technology Strategy with Self-Organising Industry Investment Boards", roneo, Berkeley.

SCHANKERMAN, M. (1991), "Measurement of the Value of Patent Rights and Inventive Output using Patent Renewal Data", *STI Review,* No. 8, OECD, Paris.

STOKES, Donald (1993), *Pasteur's Quadrant: A Study in Policy Science Ideas,* The Brookings Institution (forthcoming).

STONEMAN, Paul (1991), "The Use of a Levy/Grant System as an Alternative to Tax Based Incentives to R&D", *Research Policy 20,* pp. 195-201.

SWENSON, C.W. (1992), "Some Tests of the Incentive Effects of the Research and Experimentation Tax Credit", *Journal of Public Economics 40,* pp. 203-218.

TANAKA, M. (1989), "Japanese-style Evaluation Systems for R&D Projects: The MITI Experience", *Research Policy 18.*

TARASOFSKY, A. (1984), *The Subsidisation of Innovation Projects by the Government of Canada,* Economic Council of Canada.

TOULEMONDE, J. (1990), *L'Évaluation des effets économiques des programmes de recherche de la Communauté européenne,* EC 1990 (available only in French, with English abstract), Brussels.

TSIPOURI, L.J. (1991), "Effects of EC R&D Policy on Greece: Some Thoughts in View of the STRIDE Programme", *Scientometrics,* Vol. 21, No. 3.

TYSON, Laura D'Andrea (1992), *Who's Bashing Whom? Trade Conflict in High-Technology Industries,* Institute for International Economics, Washington DC.

WATKINS, Tod A. (1991), "A Technological Communications Costs Model of R&D Consortia as Public Policy", *Research Policy 20,* pp. 87-107.

WILLIAMS, R. (1992), "Choosing Big Technologies: The Core Issues", *History and Technology,* Vol. 9, pp. 223-234.

MAIN SALES OUTLETS OF OECD PUBLICATIONS
PRINCIPAUX POINTS DE VENTE DES PUBLICATIONS DE L'OCDE

ARGENTINA – ARGENTINE
Carlos Hirsch S.R.L.
Galería Güemes, Florida 165, 4° Piso
1333 Buenos Aires   Tel. (1) 331.1787 y 331.2391
Telefax: (1) 331.1787

AUSTRALIA – AUSTRALIE
D.A. Information Services
648 Whitehorse Road, P.O.B 163
Mitcham, Victoria 3132   Tel. (03) 873.4411
Telefax: (03) 873.5679

AUSTRIA – AUTRICHE
Gerold & Co.
Graben 31
Wien I   Tel. (0222) 533.50.14
Telefax: (0222) 512.47.31.29

BELGIUM – BELGIQUE
Jean De Lannoy
Avenue du Roi 202
B-1060 Bruxelles   Tel. (02) 538.51.69/538.08.41
Telefax: (02) 538.08.41

CANADA
Renouf Publishing Company Ltd.
1294 Algoma Road
Ottawa, ON K1B 3W8   Tel. (613) 741.4333
Telefax: (613) 741.5439
Stores:
61 Sparks Street
Ottawa, ON K1P 5R1   Tel. (613) 238.8985
211 Yonge Street
Toronto, ON M5B 1M4   Tel. (416) 363.3171
Telefax: (416)363.59.63

Les Éditions La Liberté Inc.
3020 Chemin Sainte-Foy
Sainte-Foy, PQ G1X 3V6   Tel. (418) 658.3763
Telefax: (418) 658.3763

Federal Publications Inc.
165 University Avenue, Suite 701
Toronto, ON M5H 3B8   Tel. (416) 860.1611
Telefax: (416) 860.1608

Les Publications Fédérales
1185 Université
Montréal, QC H3B 3A7   Tel. (514) 954.1633
Telefax: (514) 954.1635

CHINA – CHINE
China National Publications Import
Export Corporation (CNPIEC)
16 Gongti E. Road, Chaoyang District
P.O. Box 88 or 50
Beijing 100704 PR   Tel. (01) 506.6688
Telefax: (01) 506.3101

CHINESE TAIPEI – TAIPEI CHINOIS
Good Faith Worldwide Int'l. Co. Ltd.
9th Floor, No. 118, Sec. 2
Chung Hsiao E. Road
Taipei   Tel. (02) 391.7396/391.7397
Telefax: (02) 394.9176

CZECH REPUBLIC – RÉPUBLIQUE TCHÈQUE
Artia Pegas Press Ltd.
Narodni Trida 25
POB 825
111 21 Praha 1   Tel. 26.65.68
Telefax: 26.20.81

DENMARK – DANEMARK
Munksgaard Book and Subscription Service
35, Nørre Søgade, P.O. Box 2148
DK-1016 København K   Tel. (33) 12.85.70
Telefax: (33) 12.93.87

EGYPT – ÉGYPTE
Middle East Observer
41 Sherif Street
Cairo   Tel. 392.6919
Telefax: 360-6804

FINLAND – FINLANDE
Akateeminen Kirjakauppa
Keskuskatu 1, P.O. Box 128
00100 Helsinki

Subscription Services/Agence d'abonnements :
P.O. Box 23
00371 Helsinki   Tel. (358 0) 12141
Telefax: (358 0) 121.4450

FRANCE
OECD/OCDE
Mail Orders/Commandes par correspondance:
2, rue André-Pascal
75775 Paris Cedex 16   Tel. (33-1) 45.24.82.00
Telefax: (33-1) 49.10.42.76
Telex: 640048 OCDE

Orders via Minitel, France only/
Commandes par Minitel, France exclusivement :
36 15 OCDE

OECD Bookshop/Librairie de l'OCDE :
33, rue Octave-Feuillet
75016 Paris   Tel. (33-1) 45.24.81.81
(33-1) 45.24.81.67

Documentation Française
29, quai Voltaire
75007 Paris   Tel. 40.15.70.00

Gibert Jeune (Droit-Économie)
6, place Saint-Michel
75006 Paris   Tel. 43.25.91.19

Librairie du Commerce International
10, avenue d'Iéna
75016 Paris   Tel. 40.73.34.60

Librairie Dunod
Université Paris-Dauphine
Place du Maréchal de Lattre de Tassigny
75016 Paris   Tel. (1) 44.05.40.13

Librairie Lavoisier
11, rue Lavoisier
75008 Paris   Tel. 42.65.39.95

Librairie L.G.D.J. - Montchrestien
20, rue Soufflot
75005 Paris   Tel. 46.33.89.85

Librairie des Sciences Politiques
30, rue Saint-Guillaume
75007 Paris   Tel. 45.48.36.02

P.U.F.
49, boulevard Saint-Michel
75005 Paris   Tel. 43.25.83.40

Librairie de l'Université
12a, rue Nazareth
13100 Aix-en-Provence   Tel. (16) 42.26.18.08

Documentation Française
165, rue Garibaldi
69003 Lyon   Tel. (16) 78.63.32.23

Librairie Decitre
29, place Bellecour
69002 Lyon   Tel. (16) 72.40.54.54

Librairie Sauramps
Le Triangle
34967 Montpellier Cedex 2   Tel. (16) 67.58.85.15
Tekefax: (16) 67.58.27.36

GERMANY – ALLEMAGNE
OECD Publications and Information Centre
August-Bebel-Allee 6
D-53175 Bonn   Tel. (0228) 959.120
Telefax: (0228) 959.12.17

GREECE – GRÈCE
Librairie Kauffmann
Mavrokordatou 9
106 78 Athens   Tel. (01) 32.55.321
Telefax: (01) 32.30.320

HONG-KONG
Swindon Book Co. Ltd.
Astoria Bldg. 3F
34 Ashley Road, Tsimshatsui
Kowloon, Hong Kong   Tel. 2376.2062
Telefax: 2376.0685

HUNGARY – HONGRIE
Euro Info Service
Margitsziget, Európa Ház
1138 Budapest   Tel. (1) 111.62.16
Telefax: (1) 111.60.61

ICELAND – ISLANDE
Mál Mog Menning
Laugavegi 18, Pósthólf 392
121 Reykjavik   Tel. (1) 552.4240
Telefax: (1) 562.3523

INDIA – INDE
Oxford Book and Stationery Co.
Scindia House
New Delhi 110001   Tel. (11) 331.5896/5308
Telefax: (11) 332.5993
17 Park Street
Calcutta 700016   Tel. 240832

INDONESIA – INDONÉSIE
Pdii-Lipi
P.O. Box 4298
Jakarta 12042   Tel. (21) 573.34.67
Telefax: (21) 573.34.67

IRELAND – IRLANDE
Government Supplies Agency
Publications Section
4/5 Harcourt Road
Dublin 2   Tel. 661.31.11
Telefax: 475.27.60

ISRAEL
Praedicta
5 Shatner Street
P.O. Box 34030
Jerusalem 91430   Tel. (2) 52.84.90/1/2
Telefax: (2) 52.84.93

R.O.Y. International
P.O. Box 13056
Tel Aviv 61130   Tel. (3) 49.61.08
Telefax: (3) 544.60.39

Palestinian Authority/Middle East:
INDEX Information Services
P.O.B. 19502
Jerusalem   Tel. (2) 27.12.19
Telefax: (2) 27.16.34

ITALY – ITALIE
Libreria Commissionaria Sansoni
Via Duca di Calabria 1/1
50125 Firenze   Tel. (055) 64.54.15
Telefax: (055) 64.12.57
Via Bartolini 29
20155 Milano   Tel. (02) 36.50.83

Editrice e Libreria Herder
Piazza Montecitorio 120
00186 Roma   Tel. 679.46.28
Telefax: 678.47.51

Libreria Hoepli
Via Hoepli 5
20121 Milano   Tel. (02) 86.54.46
Telefax: (02) 805.28.86

Libreria Scientifica
Dott. Lucio de Biasio 'Aeiou'
Via Coronelli, 6
20146 Milano   Tel. (02) 48.95.45.52
Telefax: (02) 48.95.45.48

JAPAN – JAPON
OECD Publications and Information Centre
Landic Akasaka Building
2-3-4 Akasaka, Minato-ku
Tokyo 107   Tel. (81.3) 3586.2016
Telefax: (81.3) 3584.7929

KOREA – CORÉE
Kyobo Book Centre Co. Ltd.
P.O. Box 1658, Kwang Hwa Moon
Seoul   Tel. 730.78.91
Telefax: 735.00.30

OECD PUBLICATIONS, 2 rue André-Pascal, 75775 PARIS CEDEX 16
PRINTED IN FRANCE
(92 95 05 1) ISBN 92-64-14423-4 - No. 47879 1995